Aga Khan Award for Architecture

Lars Müller Publishers

Madinat al-Zahra Museum Cordoba, Spain

Foreword
Farrokh Derakhshani

Too often, the successes and failures of architecture, planning, landscape architecture and urban design—or any other projects that alter our natural and built environments—are never transmitted. We build as if we have no history and no future. Yet this information is of utmost importance if we are to avoid the destruction of what nature has bequeathed and what our ancestors constructed. If we are to create a better future, we need to learn these lessons.

One way to ensure that this information is transmitted is through the critical evaluation of projects in ways that uncover best practices. The aim is to create a sharper awareness of the aesthetic, cultural and social aspects of architecture among those who commission, those who build and those who use these projects, leading to a recognition of the deeper, "implicate" order that is inherent in the visible architectural project. This notion of the implicate and the explicate order is presented in the introduction by Mohsen Mostafavi.

Since 1980, select groups of architects, planners, artists and social scientists have convened every three years to examine a diverse selection of recently completed projects presented to them through the Aga Khan Award for Architecture. One of the main aims of this exercise is to highlight success stories.

In the 2010 Cycle, 401 projects were presented to the independent Award Master Jury, from which jury members selected a shortlist of 19 projects for in-depth review. The Award's Steering Committee —which sets the priorities for each triennial cycle—emphasised its desire for greater transparency in the selection process, and consequently the shortlist was released to the public for the first time. This created dialogue and discussion in both professional and public circles. After the On-Site Reviews and further analysis by the jury, five projects were selected to receive the 2010 Aga Khan Award for Architecture.

In this book, all 19 shortlisted projects are presented, grouped under five themes: environment, institutions, industry, dwellings and conservation. The issues they raise are further analysed from different perspectives in a series of essays. What they all share is the high level of interaction and discussion that occurred among the people who envisaged, realised and use these projects, as well as the exceptional processes of their creation.

The selection of projects for the 2010 Award started with a statement by the Steering Committee—presented to the Master Jury at the beginning of their mandate—outlining concerns about the status of the current built environment. The jury's response is manifest in their choice of projects but also in their report, which challenges many of the assumptions commonly held by professionals and decision makers today.

The final section of the book is dedicated to Oleg Grabar, the distinguished art and architectural historian and recipient of the 2010 Chairman's Award, given in recognition of lifetime achievement. The awarding of this honour does not fall under the Master Jury's mandate, but is the choice of the Steering Committee. Professor Grabar was one of the first individuals to be called on by His Highness the Aga Khan in 1977, when he established the Aga Khan Award for Architecture.

Since that time, the Aga Khan's efforts to engage with the challenges faced by the natural and built environments have grown to encompass 11 major institutions, all designed to address issues that affect the quality of life. Other agencies focus on particular development issues, from economic development to culture, and from deforestation to university education. Common to all of these initiatives is a commitment to stimulating positive change. Like the other institutions of the Aga Khan Development Network, the Award aims to provide sparks of hope and models for action. With the natural and built environments under increasing threat, these messages have become ever more urgent.

Contents

Introduction
- 4 **Foreword** Farrokh Derakhshani
- 10 **The Implicate Order of Architecture** Mohsen Mostafavi
- 18 **Steering Committee Statement**
- 22 **Master Jury Report**

- 28 **Environment**
- 30 **Wadi Hanifa Wetlands** Riyadh, Saudi Arabia
- 44 **AUB Campus Master Plan** Beirut, Lebanon

- 54 **Institution**
- 56 **Madinat al-Zahra Museum** Cordoba, Spain
- 72 **Bridge School** Xiashi Village, China
- 90 **Women's Health Centre** Ouagadougou, Burkina Faso
- 98 **Green School** Bali, Indonesia
- 108 **Chandgaon Mosque** Chittagong, Bangladesh
- 120 **Nishorgo Oirabot Nature Interpretation Centre** Teknaf, Bangladesh

- 132 **Industry**
- 134 **Ipekyol Textile Factory** Edirne, Turkey
- 150 **Restoration of Rubber Smokehouse** Kedah, Malaysia

- 158 **Dwelling**
- 160 **Tulou Collective Housing** Guangzhou, China
- 172 **Palmyra House** Alibagh, India
- 184 **Dowlat II Residential Building** Tehran, Iran
- 194 **Yodakandyia Community Centre** Hambantota District, Sri Lanka
- 202 **Reconstruction of Ngibikan Village** Yogyakarta, Indonesia

- 210 **Conservation**
- 212 **Revitalisation of the Hypercentre of Tunis** Tunisia
- 228 **Souk Waqif** Doha, Qatar
- 238 **Conservation of Gjirokastra** Albania
- 248 **Rehabilitation of Al-Karaouine Mosque** Fez, Morocco

In this colour:
Recipients of 2010 Aga Khan Award for Architecture

263 **Essays**
264 **The Shortlist** Omar Abdulaziz Hallaj
269 **Some Reflections on Postcolonial Modernity / Postcolonial Realities and Architecture of the Muslim World** Salah M. Hassan
274 **On Advocacy** Omar Abdulaziz Hallaj
276 **On-Site Review: Excursions into Ethnographic Architectural Criticism** Gökhan Karakuş
282 **Landscape as Ecological Infrastructure for an Alternative Urbanity** Yu Kongjian
286 **Reuniting Processes and Product: Lessons for the Built Environment** Hanif Kara
292 **What About Symbols?** Farshid Moussavi
300 **Walking Lightly on Earth** Souleymane Bachir Diagne
303 **Hope** Alice Rawsthorn

304 Chairman's Award
306 **Oleg Grabar**
322 **Oleg Grabar's Other Biography** Mohammad al-Asad
325 **On Knowledge and Education** Oleg Grabar
328 **The Role of the Historian** Oleg Grabar
334 **Curriculum Vitae**

336 **Award Recipients, Project Data**
342 **Shortlisted Projects, Project Data**
344 **2010 Steering Committee, Master Jury**
345 **2010 On-Site Reviewers**
348 **Awards 1980–2010**
350 **Acknowledgements**

Revitalisation of the Hypercentre of Tunis Tunisia

The Implicate Order of Architecture
Mohsen Mostafavi

Good buildings, landscapes and cities provide the physical setting for inspired human action. They frame, facilitate and enhance our daily lives in the same way that badly designed buildings, landscapes and cities hinder our constructive participation. This book is about a variety of projects across culturally diverse portions of the globe that instantiate the desire for positive change. What these projects have in common is a commitment to design excellence despite constraints of budget, resources, climate, technology and politics. They share this commitment as one of the necessary tools for societal betterment.

For the Aga Khan Award for Architecture, design excellence is not limited to the aesthetic and formal aspects of a project; it is the combination of advances made in disciplinary knowledge and the spatial qualities and everyday performance of a building that sets the preconditions for design excellence. Disciplinary advancement in architecture incorporates many issues including aesthetic, sensory, technical, formal, structural, material and cultural concerns. Equally, the concept of spatial performance is based on a deeper understanding of buildings and their use. It transcends mere technical performance and attempts to present buildings, landscapes and cities more broadly as the location of human activity and habits. This is the reason for the emphasis of the Award on social improvement through design excellence.

Small projects often have a major impact within a community, and this fact accounts for the scalar variations as well as the diversity of projects selected in this cycle of the Award. Modest endeavours take their place next to ambitious undertakings. The Award is keen to acknowledge the value and beauty of these artefacts and to recognise the need for a multiscalar approach towards reshaping the environment. Large-scale interventions, including landscapes and master-planning initiatives, are complemented by relatively small, locally focused and effective projects as mechanisms for change. Our future urban environments will need to systematically consider this type of innovative combination of top-down and bottom-up approaches to planning. This also goes hand in hand with the value of private and public collaborations as a means of creating alternative forms of urban and rural developments.

At the architectural level, it is worth pointing out that the Aga Khan Award is not specifically an award for Islamic architecture. It does not seek to identify and valorise stylistic tendencies consistent with the imagery of Islamic architecture. Instead it places emphasis on the plurality of Muslim communities and their resultant physical environments, in particular the design qualities of each project and how it achieves its intended purpose. This latter criterion cannot be judged simply on the basis of the material provided by a nominated project's designers, though Award consideration does require the submittal of a comprehensive body of both visual and written documentation.

The Aga Khan Award for Architecture is unique in its procedures of evaluation, which are designed to reflect its intellectual, technical and social aspirations. Its evaluation mechanisms are tripartite and include the participation of a Steering Committee, a Master Jury, and a team of technical or expert reviewers. The Steering Committee, working closely with His Highness the Aga Khan and the directorate for the Award, provides intellectual as well as thematic continuity from one triannual Award cycle to the next. They nominate members of the Master Jury and engage them in dialogue throughout the process of project selection and evaluation.

The Master Jury is made up of a diversity of practitioners and scholars. It tends to include a combination of architects, landscape architects, urban designers, artists and academics with a deep knowledge of Islamic culture and Muslim societies. The varied backgrounds and traditions—both Western and non-Western—represented by the Master Jury help to create an unusual and dynamic milieu for the selection of shortlisted projects.

The projects are then visited by On-Site Reviewers who evaluate their various qualities, from design to construction to use. Their report to the Master Jury includes an assessment of each project's post-occupancy performance. These evaluations also address the relation of each shortlisted project to its larger environmental and social context. They help the jury to comprehend the values of each project as a dynamic and evolving spatial artefact. In many respects, the on-site visits help present the actual circumstances of each project for the jury. This process intertwines design with its consequences; the perception of a project becomes more than its visual documentation. Each jury member has to reconcile her or his assessment and appreciation of a shortlisted project with those provided by the technical reviewer and in discussion with other jury members. This dynamic and multilayered evaluation process transforms the perceptions of jury members. The conversations and negotiations of the Master Jury change the way we consider questions of aesthetic experience and beauty, and force us to reevaluate how we judge design projects.

•

> For all beauty which is suitable and goodness which one perceives, that one loves and desires, the principle of perceiving them relies on the senses, imagination, the estimative faculty, conjecture and the intellect.
> —Ibn Sina, *Kitāb al-najā*[1]

These reflections from Avicenna, the 11th-century polymath physician and philosopher, make it clear that our appreciation of things is a complex process that requires the use of multiple human faculties. It seeks a sensibility that is an indispensable part of the understanding of beauty and "the goodness which one perceives". This shift in perception is at the heart both of the principles of the Award and of understanding others. The thoroughness of the selection process introduces a slower, more patient mode of reflection that provides the possibility for reconsidering one's preferences, prejudices and assumptions. The Aga Khan Award for Architecture therefore is an exercise in pluralism as the "embrace of multiple subjects, methods and truths".[2]

Although the idea of Islamic architecture as a stylistic tendency is not a goal of the Award, the above circumstances, including a thorough multi-style selection process, enable other possibilities. The process seeks to find alternative ways in which the design culture and sensibilities associated with Islamic architecture could locate their contemporary equivalence and the impetus for innovation.

It is, for example, well known that Islamic architecture does not promote the use of figurative representational techniques. Yet there is a rich tradition of interplay between structure, geometry and ornament, especially in the use of calligraphy, that forms the basis for the appearance of many significant buildings. The use of such abstractions produces its own evocative conditions between a building's surface and its form. The rhythms, proportions and measures of the building incorporate regimes of light and shade, hot and cold, wet and dry that make them sensorial catalysts. Think of the spaces of the mosques along the Maidan in Isfahan or of the Alhambra in Granada. How can contemporary architecture utilise the qualities and affects of these places that are so highly dependent on the understanding and study of their environmental, topographic and cultural conditions?

The use of colour and especially of polychromatic tiles on the surfaces of many Islamic buildings is one way in which overall impact can be transmitted without resort to literal visual references. The best versions of such buildings are experientially charged places, powerful spatial constructs, rather than structures apprehended only through the direct communicability of their facades. The Aga Khan Award for Architecture promotes the application of this more holistic sensibility in appraising all types of buildings.

If in designing buildings for Muslim communities we should learn from Islamic architecture without directly copying it, then what can we learn from Islamic cities? The dense fabric of many Islamic cities —with their rich traditions of houses, streets, markets and religious and secular public buildings and public spaces, as well as their social and organisational structures such as the *waqf*—provides an important reference point for the planning of contemporary Muslim communities. In the absence of an overall sense of the city, many new examples of urban development, from Dubai to Pudong, follow a model of urbanisation that is based primarily on the development of large individual building plots by what are essentially private companies. What these developments generally lack is any systematic articulation of public infrastructure and sense of connection to a programmatically rich ground specifically designed for the benefit of the urban dweller. The best examples of Islamic cities from Aleppo to Cairo also provide models of sustainable development. The compactness and adjacencies of buildings within Islamic cities create an economical use of land as well as thermally efficient construction. The easy and economical availability of local materials further contributes to the sustainable character of traditional Islamic cities. What can we learn from such urban precedents without having to resort to nostalgic and kitschy replication?

One possible exception is Masdar, an experiment in building a large-scale sustainable community in Abu Dhabi. Only a fraction of this project is currently under construction, so it will be years before anyone will have the opportunity to evaluate its genuine success. Yet such efforts do provide important avenues for research and development. Masdar is capable of providing alternative modes of contemporary construction that pay homage to the environmental qualities of Islamic cities without directly imitating them. But the ethos of such bounded communities, like those of most new towns, involves as much social engineering as it does real engineering. This makes it imperative for the client and the designers to constantly negotiate the reciprocal relations between the technical and the social, the planned and the unexpected (even if welcomed). For that to occur, the development of these types of communities would have to be as cognisant of their social, political and economic potentials and differences as they are of their architecture.

•

In previous cycles of the Award, only the small group of premiated projects were announced publicly. During this cycle, the decision was made to present the full list of all projects shortlisted for On-Site Review by the Master Jury. This new approach has been helpful in revealing the diversity of project types and regions represented by more than 400 nominated projects, ranging from houses to housing, a health care facility, a community centre, a museum, a factory, landscapes, a university campus, schools and many conservation and restoration projects. The projects come from equally diverse geographic locations, including Saudi Arabia, Lebanon, Albania, China, Bangladesh, Spain, Iran and Malaysia.

This year also marks a rare occasion when the Steering Committee, under the guidance of His Highness, presents the prestigious Chairman's Award. Oleg Grabar, one of the world's leading scholars of Islamic art and architecture, is only the fourth recipient of this honour, and it is the first time that a historian has been so recognised for his contribution to the field. Grabar, probably more than any other scholar, has paved the way for a deeper understanding of the arts within Muslim communities—a tradition that continues to grow with the work of many of his former students.

The contributions of Grabar and of the nominated projects constitute a world, a collective of sorts, with many intellectual and cultural overlaps and affiliations. It is certainly true that the projects have been judged on their individual merits. But they are also part of cities, communities and territories with diverse populations and habits of mind. In fact, all projects featured in this book—whether a house, a school, a landscape or a factory—constitute specific places within neighbourhoods and communities of participation, and shape their citizens' democratic ideals. Seen from afar, the network of these distinct localities, despite their geographic distance, provides a sense of connection and proximity, as if they were all part of some imagined yet illusory analogical city.

Such a city requires many buildings by and for various stakeholders —private and public, commercial and institutional, including offices and workshops, plazas and parks. These are also the types of projects that the Aga Khan Award for Architecture seeks for nomination and recognition: projects that oscillate between the everyday and the unique. The premiated projects are exemplars of this intention, and as such are explicitly assessed in terms of their design as well as their social benefits, and more implicitly in terms of their contribution to a set of aspirational and spatial ideals of urban as well as rural communities.

The shortlisted projects for the Aga Khan Award as the designed artefacts of a city contribute to the network of urban interactions and result in the productive generation of additional social effects. These networks today operate at the scale of the territory. They are not simply bounded and static but dynamic and mobile, physical and virtual. The consequence of this approach towards the urban territory is a greater appreciation of the regional scale of urban development. The city and the surrounding territories are seen as part of an evolving and interconnected process.

The important yet underappreciated and controversial American physicist David Bohm, writing in the 1970s and 1980s, proposed a new notion of order that he called the implicate and the explicate. Bohm's ideas challenged the convention of seeing the world as a series of separate, indivisible and unchangeable particles or "building blocks". Instead his work focused on the importance of the "undivided whole" or the implicate order inherent within the whole. In this view, nothing is separate or totally autonomous. Of course Bohm was not thinking of architecture or the urban environment when he developed his theories. In fact, he was more concerned with the incompatibility of quantum theory with relativity theory.

> In relativity, movement is continuous, causally determinate and well defined, while in quantum mechanics it is discontinuous, not causally determinate and not well defined. Each theory is committed to its own notions of essentially static and fragmentary modes of existence. . . . One thus sees that a new kind of theory is needed which drops these basic commitments and at most recovers some essential features of the older theories as abstract forms derived from a deeper reality in which what prevails is unbroken wholeness.[3]

But the implicate notion of "unbroken wholeness" is the context within which "relative autonomy" or the explicate order exists. By analogy, what architects and designers do through their work are explicate demonstrations. These demonstrations—buildings—operate in relation to the implicate order. In architectural terms, the former is by definition visible (explicate) while the latter is at least in part invisible (implicate). In terms of the Award, the links between the visible order of a project—its built reality—and its less visible, situational and contingent circumstances are also key aspects of the relational condition of architecture that affect not only its formation but also its performance and reception.

Each architectural, landscape or urban project exists in this constant state of both unfoldment (the singularity of its realised and visible manifestation) and enfoldment into the wholeness—for example, that of the urban as the social, political, symbolic and cultural context for the implicate order of architecture. The Aga Khan Award recognises the value of the productive tension between these two states: the relative autonomy of a project and its entanglement within a more complex matrix of forces that sustain its enabling capacities for public good. This is one of the indispensable benefits of the Aga Khan Award for Architecture.

Notes
1 Ibn Sina, *Kitāb al-najā*, edited by Majid Fakhri (Beirut, 1985), p. 282.
2 Timothy Snyder, "On Tony Judt", *The New York Review of Books*, October 14, 2010.
3 David Bohm, *Wholeness and the Implicate Order* (London: Routledge, 1980), p. xv.

Bridge School Xiashi Village, China

Steering Committee Statement
2010 Award Cycle

In the pursuit of architectural excellence, the Aga Khan Award for Architecture has premiated a range of projects that have addressed crucial issues for Muslim communities. These include problems of identity and pluralism in a world marked by the forces of globalisation, while preserving the importance of heritage, memory and a sense of place. Since its inception, the Award has promoted successful interventions in the built environment and has contributed to social and economic developments committed to establishing equity. In all instances, the Award has adhered to the highest standards of architectural practice. At the same time, it has recognised approaches that challenge and expand existing boundaries, whether technical, professional or conceptual. These are all issues that have a continuing significance for the deliberations of the Master Jury.

Since the 1990s, the Award has extended such explorations to new frontiers. It has acknowledged buildings that address environmental and climatic challenges, and has engaged with issues affecting the urban scale. Historic preservation and poverty alleviation have been recognised as pressing issues in previous cycles. New boundaries for urbanism were explored, ranging from the use of reforestation to provide cities with greenbelts, to initiatives in urban planning and preservation in the service of developing confidence and trust between conflicting communities.

The Award has a pluralistic and generous perspective that engages with projects that contribute to the transformation of the quality of life for Muslim communities in various settings, whether urban or rural, national or diasporic. One of the challenging issues presented by projects nominated for the 11th Cycle is whether their specific relevance to Muslim societies extends to a broader significance for diverse communities in countries with emerging economies. In this context, the jury may well want to reflect upon which of these developments affecting architecture and the built environment are of particular relevance to Muslim peoples in a transnational world.

A related issue would be to define those features of a project that may directly bear on the lives of Muslim peoples who may have a significant presence within a multicultural community without forming a majority. In the absence of such criteria, the Award risks losing its primary aim, which is to establish standards and practices of architectural excellence that contribute to the well-being and advancement of Muslim societies.

Muslim communities throughout the world are facing mounting challenges relating to the quality of their built environments, which makes this continuous process of reexamination and redefinition an ongoing priority. Environmental concerns are becoming increasingly critical as levels of air, water and soil pollution, as well as shortages of water resources, reach grave proportions. Many urban centres are undergoing serious and continuous deterioration as a result of the mounting pressures of rapidly increasing populations and crumbling infrastructures. This is evident in a multiplicity of urban problems including overcrowding, sprawl and overwhelming levels of traffic congestion.

The Award needs to continue to identify innovative types of interventions in the built environment, while recognising imaginative responses to traditional forms of architecture. In order to engage with these challenges, the Award proposes an integrated approach to architectural best practice and its relationship to the quality of life for the populations it serves. Master planning projects, public transportation solutions, and infrastructural initiatives are a high priority for the Award. Industrial sites and places of work have been carefully considered with a view to providing architectural excellence in the shaping of public spaces that cater to merchandising and leisure activities. Such a generous interpretation of the built environment must place a high premium on issues of economic opportunity that profoundly affect the welfare and security of vulnerable communities.

The Award is particularly concerned with the long-standing neglect of rural societies that has intensified in the age of globalisation. Architectural and planning solutions could greatly contribute to the alleviation of such conditions of distress in rural environments. This is a challenge for all those involved in the decision-making process. Government officials, planners and engineers must share the responsibility for protecting and improving the built environment with community leaders, clients and consumers. All of them need to come up with creative solutions for dealing with serious challenges to society and improving upon the quality of life currently available to populations across the world.

While it seems unlikely that any individual project could deal with all of the issues we have proposed for your consideration, we hope that the projects identified for premiation by the Master Jury will take a thoughtful approach to some of the threshold criteria that we have identified above.

Geneva, 13 January 2010

Ipekyol Textile Factory Edirne, Turkey

Master Jury Report
2010 Award Cycle

The intersection of identity and pluralism in a globalised world, where memory, heritage and belonging are threatened, emerged as central concerns during the jury debates. Since its inception, the Award has striven to explore new frontiers while maintaining a generous and pluralistic perspective, engaging projects that contribute to the transformation and improvement of the quality of the built environment. It has considered projects of significance both to the Islamic world and to multicultural societies in which Muslims represent a minority or an expansion of new or historic diasporas. We understood our task as being to engage those projects which respond to the mounting challenges facing Muslim societies or societies where Muslims have a significant presence, ranging from environmental issues, neglect of rural communities, rapid industrialisation and deterioration of urban infrastructure to concerns about heritage and memory in the broadest sense. As a jury, we remained mindful of promoting the most successful interventions in the built environment, while ensuring that they set the highest standards of excellence.

While reviewing the 401 nominated projects (19 of which were shortlisted and 5 selected as Award recipients), the jury had the opportunity to survey a broad range of themes and trends. As a jury, we did not prejudice our selection by any prior definition of an agenda, but remained sensitive to priorities brought to the surface by our review of the work of practitioners and stakeholders in the built environment everywhere, broadening our scope both in and outside the Islamic world.

The Award-winning projects represent the diversity of the Muslim world and its diasporas, as well as being innovative in their own right. In the jury deliberations, specific themes emerged which defined our understanding of the scope of the Award.

First, ecologically sound projects in conception and implementation which demonstrated sensitivity to environmental concerns emerged as preferred models for replication in urban contexts and in alleviating ecological problems. They can provide alternative social spaces for urban populations and counterbalance the proliferation of malls and shopping centres as central spaces for entertainment.

At the technological level, innovations in providing ecological alternatives for the recycling of water while addressing natural seasonal problems such as floods were also recognised as crucial.

Second, projects aiming at the preservation and reclamation of recent heritage, associated with the colonial period, highlighted the role of urban centres in former European colonies as sites of experimentation with modernism, and their centrality in a reconsideration of global modernities. Several of the shortlisted projects highlighted the importance of promoting civil initiatives which are sensitive to issues of funding, the revitalisation of local economies and their role in providing opportunities for local employment and training.

Third, there was an understanding that enlightened design is crucial in the development of safe and efficient workplaces, and that the worst effects of an industrialising world can be avoided. Such a need, for workers and management alike, was identified as of utmost priority in a time of rapid industrialisation in the Muslim world.

Fourth, the importance of building institutions for the preservation and display of cultural heritage in the context of active archaeological sites demonstrated the need for extreme sensitivity to location and historic landscape. This has been coupled with the importance of such projects in rethinking identity in Western contexts and the role of Islamic cultures and civilisation in the shaping of the European Enlightenment and modernity. Finally, the importance of looking for innovative small-scale projects as models of inserting modern structures within traditional and rural settings in a sensitive and non-intrusive manner also came to define one of the jury's criteria in identifying winning projects.

In a historically interconnected and increasingly globalised society, perceiving the world in stereotypes of separate cultural entities does not hold strong credence. Today, professional practitioners, as well as decision makers and funders, are beginning to understand the extent of the contributions of the Muslim world both geographically and historically. In a postcolonial context, culture is understood as something to be shared and cultural diversity as a value to be cherished. In this regard, the Islamic world has not only made major contributions to the narratives of global history but also to particular local histories within and outside its recognised boundaries.

The built environment is subject to rapid processes of transformation, very often backed by larger and more robust investment. In the midst of such change, concerns for the environment, for the built heritage and for the social fabric are often relegated to a secondary importance, if not neglected altogether. The shortlisted and awarded projects try to redefine priorities and emphasise a sensitive understanding of their immediate and broader contexts. Despite the great difference in their scale, context and functionality, they exhibit a responsible quality, of treading lightly on earth.

Muslims are majorities in some places, minorities in others and absent elsewhere. Globalisation should not be viewed only as an intrusion into Muslim cultures but an opportunity for diverse cultures to merge in a mutually coexisting manner. The winning projects reveal the ways in which Muslim societies are positioned to accommodate otherness as part of a process of reconciliation and conviviality. Improving the image of Muslims in a world that is both increasingly globalised and segregated is but one way this issue has been addressed. Yet also, accepting the other into the very definition of Muslim heritage is a very powerful way of addressing conviviality and multiplicity. The very definition of who is included within this collective remains problematic.

The above mentioned themes—defining the boundaries of Muslim culture in a globalising world, treading lightly on earth and conviviality—have emerged from a diligent review of projects presented. The projects brought forward the need for improving the quality of life in local communities while being capable of serving as role models for other communities in the Islamic world. They provide an ethical sensitivity to their contexts, by promoting sustainability on all fronts: environmental, social and economic. And while we understand that no one project can provide all the answers to the needs of Muslim societies, we believe that these projects collectively tell a story of hope matched with perseverance, pride tempered with humility and unity without sacrificing diversity.

Geneva, 10 June 2010

Wadi Hanifa Wetlands Riyadh, Saudi Arabia

Environment

How should we take care of, curate and design large territories? These examples transcend the scale of individual buildings. Ranging in scope from the wetlands of Wadi Hanifa in Saudi Arabia to the campus of the American University of Beirut, they demonstrate the importance of physical environments. These sites shape our activities and habits. But they also show how through design, we can nurture our surroundings and create sustainable and pleasurable environments for the benefit of diverse communities.

Wadi Hanifa Wetlands
Riyadh, Saudi Arabia

The Wadi Hanifa is a "living valley" (or "living wadi") recovered and fully integrated into the life of Riyadh. The project proposes a clean, green, safe and healthy environment, and provides continuous parkland that connects city and wadi. Combined residential development, farming, recreation, cultural activities and tourism inhabit an oasis that extends the full length of Riyadh and beyond, into the surrounding rural areas.

The Wadi Hanifa watershed is an oasis located in the heart of the Najd Plateau in the Kingdom of Saudi Arabia. Its basin and many tributaries form a unique 120-kilometre-long ecological zone that descends from the Tuwaiq escarpment in the northwest to the open desert southeast of Riyadh. For centuries, the Wadi Hanifa watershed system provided sustenance for communities along its length, where a balance prevailed between the wadi's resources, natural processes and human interventions. The Wadi Hanifa is inextricably linked to Riyadh's history.

In the late 18th century, the first Saudi state strategically located its capital at Addiriyyah on the west bank of Wadi Hanifa, taking advantage of water and arable lands. Subsequently, Riyadh (or in Arabic, Arriyadh), the new capital of the modern Saudi state, developed to the east of Wadi Hanifa and was used as a sustainable source of water and food for the city. Beginning in the early 1970s, Riyadh expanded westward towards Wadi Hanifa, and the wadi was overexploited to satisfy the increasing demand for water and mineral resources to meet the massive construction needs arising from rapid growth.

By the 1980s, Riyadh's explosive growth on the Wadi Hanifa led to the rise of ground water, dumping, environmental degradation and loss of natural functioning and ecosystem productivity. In response, in 1994 the Arriyadh Development Authority (ADA) developed the Strategy for Wadi Hanifa. But the wadi continued to deteriorate, and the ADA recognised that proper implementation of the strategy required a comprehensive and coordinated development plan, as well as a management structure to supervise it. A committee of government agencies was formed to define the wadi's flood boundaries and identify encroachments.

In 2001, the ADA commissioned the British firm Buro Happold and their Canadian landscape architect partners, Moriyama & Teshima, to develop the Wadi Hanifa Comprehensive Development Plan (WHCDP). The WHCDP was part of a 10-year programme to develop Wadi Hanifa as an environmental, recreational and tourist resource, restore its natural beauty, and rehabilitate and harness its water resources. The ADA recognised that the lack of planning controls would seriously undermine the restoration project, and an area known as the Wadi Hanifa Reserve was defined as the place where the planning policies would be applied.

The Plan was divided into two parts: The Wadi Hanifa Restoration Project to restore flood performance and water quality, and to complete the restoration of the wadi bed; and the Wadi Hanifa Development Program, focused on public infrastructure and landscape capital construction works. The works involved the removal of almost 1.25 million cubic metres of construction waste, along with inert and non-inert waste that had been dumped in the wadi over many years. There was also a restoration of the wadi channel as preparation for a 20-year flood plan. Prior to this, there had been widespread flooding due to the rubble and illegal building within the wadi.

The Bio-remediation Facility is one of the most impressive features of the project. The facility incorporates a series of weirs, riffles, pools, aerating pumps, bio-remediation cells, artificial periphyton and benthic substrates and riparian planting. Together, the elements of this design have developed the appropriate aquatic and riparian conditions to assimilate contaminants and further purify the water through a community of natural organisms that aggregate to form a food web. This has contributed to the improvement of the environmental quality of the wadi and has greatly enhanced public perception and use.

In its geographic scale, the project's ecological strategy integrates a wide range of architectural interventions, from master planning to landscaping, from architecture to signage and urban furniture. The Wadi Hanifa project aims at sustaining and protecting the environment, technically called "land building or land inhabiting", which in Arabic translates as 'Emaratul-Ard, meaning both building (architecture) and planting (landscape).

Jury Citation

This project reverses the tide of rapid urban development, which has seen public space in many cities within the Muslim world fall victim to expropriation and other practices that deprive the population of its resources. This invariably happens at the cost of environmental values and sensitive ecosystems. The Wadi Hanifa Wetlands project eloquently demonstrates an alternative ecological way of urban development. It shows how a major natural phenomenon which, through the course of urbanisation, became a litter-strewn and dangerous place—a scar on the face of the capital city—can be transformed by sensitive planning attentive to social values and imaginative infrastructure-driven landscape solutions.

The Award has been given in recognition of the project's vision and persistence in developing a sustainable environment. Using landscape as an ecological infrastructure, the project has restored and enhanced the natural systems' capacity to provide multiple services, including cleaning the contaminated water, mediating the natural forces of flood, providing habitats for biodiversity and creating opportunities for recreational, educational and aesthetic experiences.

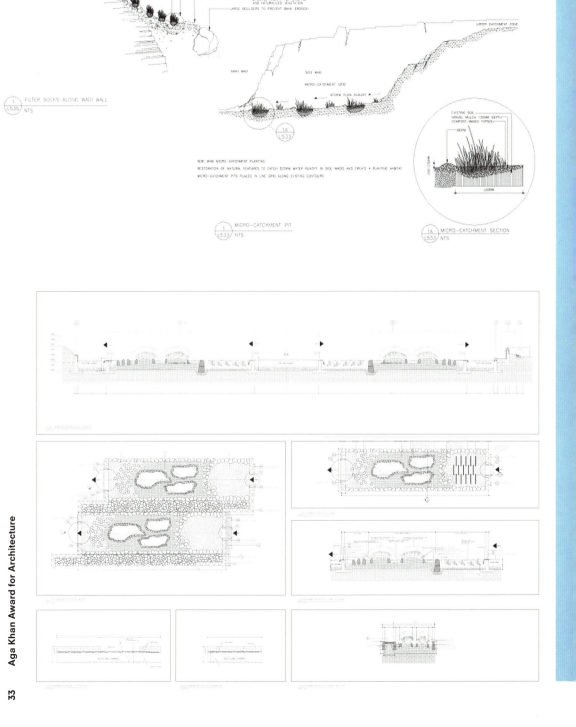

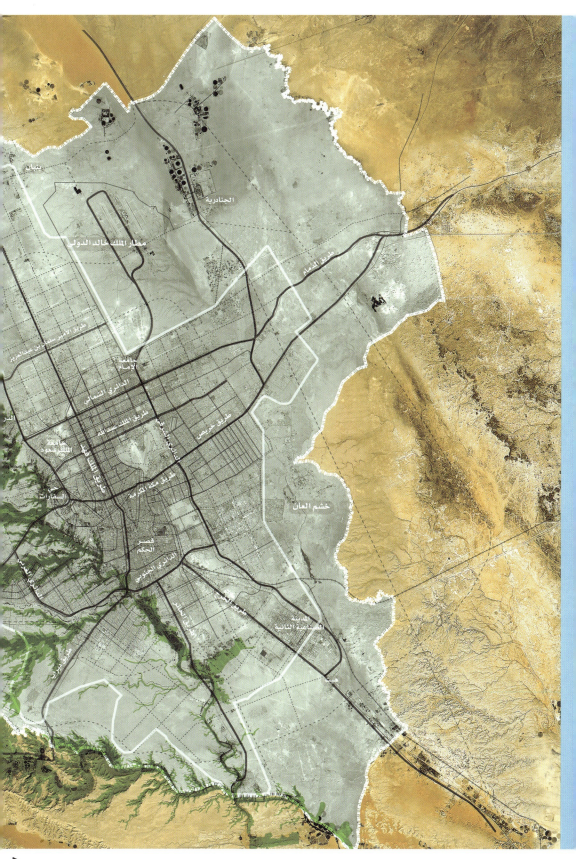

AUB Campus Master Plan
Beirut, Lebanon

In May 2002, the American University of Beirut (AUB) Master Plan to guide the physical development of the university over the next 20 years was completed. The Plan provides architectural, landscape and urban design guidelines for development of the new Olayan School of Business, the Charles Hostler Student Centre and an expanded medical campus, and includes improvements to campus infrastructure.

The Master Plan maintains the historic heritage of the upper campus with a rehabilitated medical campus, transforms the currently eclectic lower campus and enhances the middle campus, a vegetation-covered limestone escarpment. A key feature of the Plan is to develop and enhance existing and new campus districts and quadrangles. Pedestrians will replace automobiles almost everywhere, and roadways will give way to pedestrian promenades, plazas and new green spaces designed to link the three campuses and maintain the unique position of AUB between the city of Beirut and the Mediterranean Sea. Special attention is given to view corridors sweeping down from the upper campus to the sea and the mountains beyond. Situated in a high-density urban context, the campus is a focal point for its adjacent community and the city. The landscape setting is one of the most memorable and renowned aspects of the campus, and the Plan is careful not to disrupt this natural beauty and instead works to enhance and sustain it. The recommendations of the Master Plan are gradually being enacted on the campus, and some public areas have been landscaped.

Vincent James Architecture Associates designed the Charles Hostler Student Centre, which is recognised on the 2009 American Institute of Architects Top Ten Green Projects List. Machado and Silvetti Associates designed the Olayan School of Business, with a hanging facade that replicates the warmth of the local Forni limestone present throughout the campus and openings of the screenlike skin that recall the wooden *mashrabiyya* characteristic of the region.

Perhaps the most successful element in this project was the civic engagement process generating the Master Plan for this vast and complex facility. The AUB Master Plan project exemplifies a successful engagement of a large number of different end users, communities and representatives that should be followed by future large-scale projects.

Institution

Our institutions are the emblems of our collective aspirations and achievements. The Madinat al-Zahra Museum in Cordoba, Spain, or the Bridge School in Xiashi, China, are examples of positive institution building. The Bridge School both literally and metaphorically unites the two parts of a remote rural village. These and the other selected projects, including a Women's Health Centre that serves 40,000 people in Burkina Faso, enhance the intellectual, cultural and social life of their communities.

Madinat al-Zahra Museum
Cordoba, Spain

The 10th-century palace city of Madinat al-Zahra, near Cordoba, is widely considered one of the most significant early Islamic archaeological sites in the world. A provincial capital under the Romans, Cordoba was conquered by Muslim Berbers in 711, and in 756 the Damascene Umayyad dynasty emigrated to Andalusia and established the Cordoba caliphate (929–1013). The caliphate controlled most of the Iberian Peninsula and is considered the high point of Islamic rule in Spain, with Muslims, Jews and Christians contributing to its prosperity and cultural flourishing. The term *convivencia* was coined by medieval historians to describe this era of relative harmony.

In 936, Abd al-Rahman III began work on a new palace city for the caliphate 5 kilometres west of Cordoba, and 11 years later the court moved there from Cordoba. Built on a series of terraces, Madinat al-Zahra covered nearly 280 acres. The city was celebrated for its opulent cultural life, and its construction was described as "a singular moment in history, when the most vibrant intellectual and cultural force in Europe was rooted in Islam, and when the heart of Islam was in many ways rooted in Europe".[1] Suddenly, in 1010, Madinat al-Zahra was sacked in a conflict over Abd al-Rahman's succession that would bring down the Cordoban caliphate.

The archaeological remains of Madinat al-Zahra were discovered in 1911, and since then approximately 10–15 per cent of the site has been excavated. The significance of the ruins lies not only in their excellent state of preservation but in the authorship of the complex and the brevity of its history. Abd al-Rahman created the city ex nihilo, and only eight decades later the city was destroyed, never to be reinhabited. Antonio Vallejo, director of excavations for 25 years, notes that Madinat al-Zahra was the largest city ever built at one time in Western Europe. As the conception and design of a single Muslim ruler, the site represents an ideal prototype of 10th-century Islamic culture.

In the mid-1990s, Vallejo developed a master site plan with architect Juan Navarro Baldeweg to finalise the programme and provide a physical barrier to encroaching development. Infrared technology helped them locate the future museum/interpretive center at the southeast corner of the site, just outside the area of archaeological remains. The placement also has historical significance, as it marks the historical entry to the Madinat al-Zahra.

The programme included three main areas: a museum for artefacts display and site interpretation, a working area for the archaeological team and research facilities for local and visiting scholars. The architects were inspired by the agricultural countryside and buried the building in the earth to be read as part of the landscape. The building consists of a series of rectangular pavilions, with each housing a discrete programme area. The rectangular form is repeated in the landscape, and beds are planted with native olive and orange trees believed to have existed at Madinat al-Zahra. The use of the pavilion module allows for future expansion, if programme needs require. Although the building is partially submerged, natural light is assured through an exterior corridor that wraps around the building, and a series of five patios. The central patio is the building's principal organising element: to its west lies the public areas for visitors, and to the east and south are private areas for staff, archaeologists and researchers.

The architect's intent was to create a coarse building that evoked the retaining walls and temporary structures of archaeological digs. There is a restricted palette of materials, and details are direct and simple. Materials were also selected to evoke those used at Madinat al-Zahra: white concrete, suggesting the white stone walls on the site; weathered steel for doors and windows; and the monumental panel at the north end of the work yard, echoing the massive bronze doors of Cordoba's Mezquita. The small rectangular openings in walls—along the central patio, the office wing and the library wing—simulate the *mashrabiyya* effect by restricting views and modulating intense sunlight. On the inside face of these openings are single-glazed casement windows, also framed in weathered steel. The panel, doors, frames and fittings are, in essence, carpentry in steel.

Note
1   See R. McLean, "Growth in Spain Threatens a Jewel of Medieval Islam", *New York Times*, 16 August 2005.

Jury Citation

The Madinat al-Zahra Museum is a unique celebration of the link between museology and archaeology. It harmoniously and humbly blends into the landscape, understanding itself as serving the heritage being revealed in the site to which it is organically connected. This humility only adds to the powerful message it represents, one that is of particular significance in and for our times. Because the Madinat al-Zahra Museum springs out of the soil and remains incorporated within it, it presents with superb architectural eloquence the spirit of an Islamic culture which was—which is—indigenous to Spain and Europe, as it emanates from the ground itself, one of the region's multiple roots.

The Madinat al-Zahra Museum is a symbol of the *conviviencia* evoked by the name Andalusia and bears testimony that indeed, Cordoba is the future, not only the past.

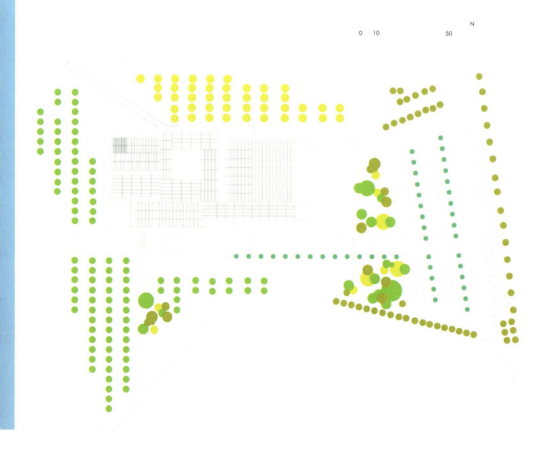

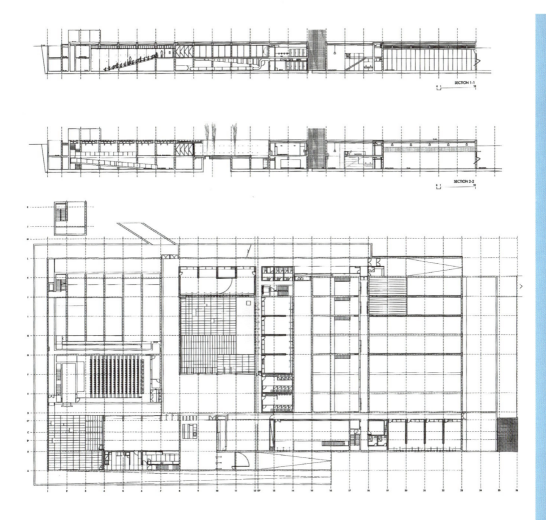

Bridge School
Xiashi, China

Xiashi is a small, 450-year-old village in China's rural Fujian province. The village is located in a hilly area and gently slopes down to the west from its entrance. It is home to 300 families and has a population of 700; the main occupation is grapefruit farming. The housing stock is changing rapidly, and the traditional earthen-walled and tiled-roofed housing, known as *tulou*, is quickly being replaced by concrete-frame structures with brick infill. Dating back approximately 400 years, the *tulou* is a fortress-like typology that housed extended families within thick, circular walls that rose up four storeys. The living quarters were located along the peripheral mud wall, and the central space was for communal use. A creek runs through the centre of the village, and there had been no crossing over it for many years.

Chen Jianshen, an architecture student from a nearby village, ventured into Xiashi while visiting his home, and he learned from the village chief that they needed a primary school. His professor, the architect Li Xiaodong, had built a school in another village that had won praise and many awards. The student approached his professor with the idea of building a Xiashi school, and he was immediately interested. The local government could not provide funds for the entire project, so the architect donated some of his own money and helped to raise the rest. His student agreed to stay in the village and supervise the construction.

The village had not designated a site for the school, and Li Xiaodong saw an opportunity in the presence of the creek and the village history of social division and stagnation. The idea of a bridge emerged. Not only could it house the simple functions required for the school but it could also physically and symbolically unify the community. The idea of a building as a bridge, although not unknown in other parts of the world, was a new concept for the community. The Bridge School creates a public space for the village, which it previously did not have, and gives new meaning to the *tulou*s by opening up views towards them—a reminder of past building traditions.

The school structure is made of two steel trusses that span the creek. Though a new technology to the village, steel was considered appropriate for its strength and economy of size, durability and ease of maintenance. The members were fabricated elsewhere and assembled on site. Each truss has three sections: the two ends that support the two classrooms and the middle section that supports the library. From each end section, cantilevered corridors slope up to the central space to access the classrooms. The school's form and circulation route shifts from one side to the other via the central space, and the classrooms are wedge-shaped with a stepped gallery floor. A small wooden stage on a steel frame cantilevers out from the northern classroom, and the southern classroom can also be reached through a sloped steel surface that the children also use as a slide. Underneath the school, a pedestrian bridge is suspended with steel cables, making an irregular pattern that gently zigzags diagonally across. The trusses transfer the load of the structure by resting on concrete bases on either side of the creek. The one on the northern side is shallow and the one to the south higher, which allows for a small shop to be nestled within it. The facade treatment of narrow timber strips helps moderate the light and keep the interior in shade.

The arrangement of the two classrooms is very simple. If compared to the standard school typology of corridor and classrooms, in this organisation, three sides of the classrooms are exposed for ample light and air flow. The architect designed minimalist classroom furniture from local pinewood; there are bookcases along the end wall, and the children sit on the gallery steps and work on wooden desks that can also become stools for adults.

The building's design is small and modern, and sensitive to the village scale. It makes no reference to traditional building styles of the area but offers a quiet and dignified presence that is striking in its simplicity.

Jury Citation

When architect Li Xiaodong was asked to build a tiny school for a small village crossed by a river, he had the inspiration of placing it on a new bridge, near the spot where two ancient *tulou* —traditional fortress-like, circular structures—were erected on either side of the river. The very modern structure not only blends successfully into the landscape, it also succeeds in joining the bulky forms of the two historic structures through a linear lightweight sculpture that floats above the river.

By placing the school on the bridge, underneath which the waters flow, the architect is giving the most important lesson a child can learn: life is transient, not one second of it similar to the next. The structure's lightness and playfulness, and its naturalness, as though it had always existed in the landscape, appeals to the children, who use it as a big toy. These qualities, and the sense of security the children feel, all come from the excellence of the architecture, from the project's concept to its smallest physical details.

The Bridge School achieves unity at many levels: temporal unity between past and present, formal unity between traditional and modern, spatial unity between the two riverbanks, social unity between one-time rival communities—as well as unity with the future.

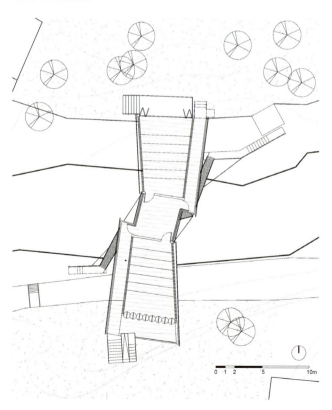

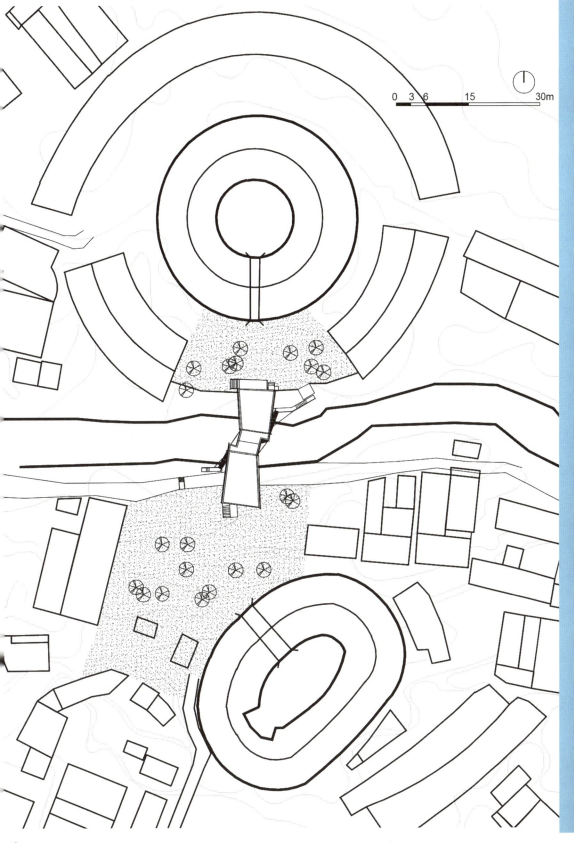

Women's Health Centre
Ouagadougou, Burkina Faso

The Centre pour le Bien-être de la Femme (CBF) is located in Sector 27 of Burkina Faso's capital Ouagadougou, one of the poorest suburbs on the city's northeastern limits. The site for the Centre is still only partially urbanised, and when land was first allocated for the project there was very little development in the area. Since then, the Centre has created a dynamic for increased urban development for its rural migrant population, and the municipality has recently built the major connecting road for the project. The CBF strives to improve women's lives and guarantee their reproductive health and sexual rights. The CBF serves the entire 40,000-person community in Sector 27, both women and men, with programmes for health, awareness and social action.

The building consists of two separate 250-square-metre blocks—a community centre and a counselling centre—placed atop an artificial plane created by a single structural platform, which is raised above grade to ensure programme-appropriate hygienic conditions, increase ventilation and protect against dust, mud and humidity. The CBF also uses a double roof strategy, with corrugated metal and acrylic sheets laid on steel I-beams, set in parallel to the width of the rooms, and supported by earth-block walls. The acrylic sheets ensure that the rooms receive indirect natural light, reducing electrical demand. The second roof is made of a 16.8-square-metre steel grid, supported by a tree-shaped steel structure and reinforced concrete columns, and covered by a recycled PVC canopy, which allows for a 90-centimetre overhang from every side of the platforms. The canopy is tightly stretched to the grid and is sloped to channel rainwater drainage. The cross-ventilation system, with a careful orientation and plentiful shaded areas, provides a significant reduction in the need for air conditioning.

The project makes innovative use of locally available materials and resources to respond in an efficient and responsible manner to climate constraints and reduce cooling needs. The project's technological and typological solutions, on a par with its social objectives, represent the formal expression of new approaches to community practices promoted by client organisations.

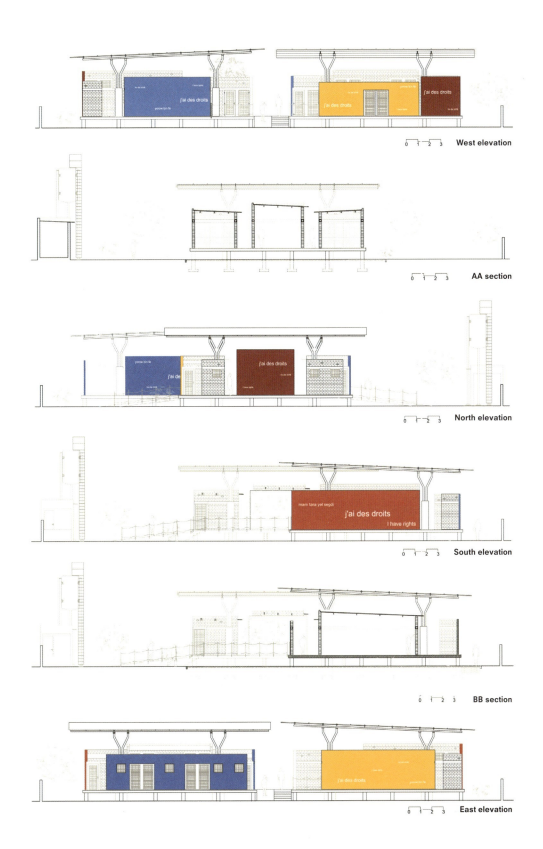

Green School
Bali, Indonesia

Throughout the island of Bali, bamboo grows everywhere. It is widely used for temporary structures at communal festivities and religious events but is not traditionally considered a material for permanent buildings. On the Green School campus, bamboo is used in structurally innovative ways to create original architectural spaces.

The Green School building typologies were very irregular, and there was little precedent for their structural analysis. The design team worked with Professor Morisco, an expert of bamboo properties at the Structural Engineering Laboratory at Yogyakarta's Gadjah Mada University, to prepare accurate computer models of the Green School buildings. From these, a structural engineering team was able to test the axial, window and earthquake loads to ensure compliance with Indonesian building codes.

Campus buildings and structures include the "Heart of School" building, which uses bamboo joints and 18-metre bamboo columns as a structural mass to support its three storeys. The Gymnasium has structural bamboo arches, which create an 18-metre column-free span 14 metres in height. The Metapantigan Studio has four main arches comprised of three bundled *petung* bamboos, also providing a column-free span. The Kul Kul Bridge, connecting both sides of the Ayung River, is a 20-metre bamboo suspension bridge that was empirically tested to support a 6-ton load. Most campus buildings do not have walls or doors, but some of the offices and faculty housing use bamboo infill panels and single glazing for enclosure. *Alang alang* thatching, a traditional roofing system made from a resilient local grass, is used for all buildings.

The School also works with the Meranggi Foundation, an environmental nonprofit organisation that raises bamboo seedlings in their campus nursery and distributes them to farmers across the island to help them grow commercially valuable bamboo species. The Foundation maintains detailed planting records using GPS technology, monitors bamboo growth rates (including associated carbon capture) and secures markets for future bamboo trade. To date, the Meranggi Foundation has distributed more than 60,000 bamboo seedlings, and within a few years they strive to generate enough bamboo for a sustainable construction industry to help supplement local farmers' income.

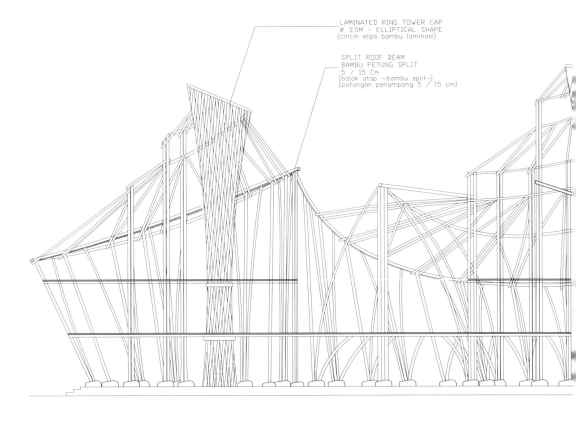

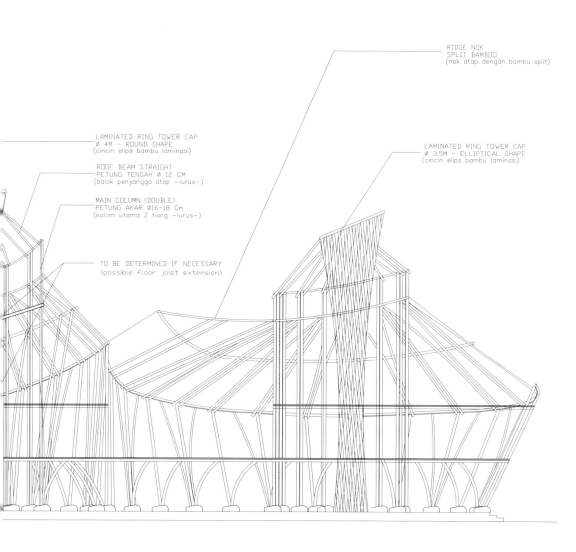

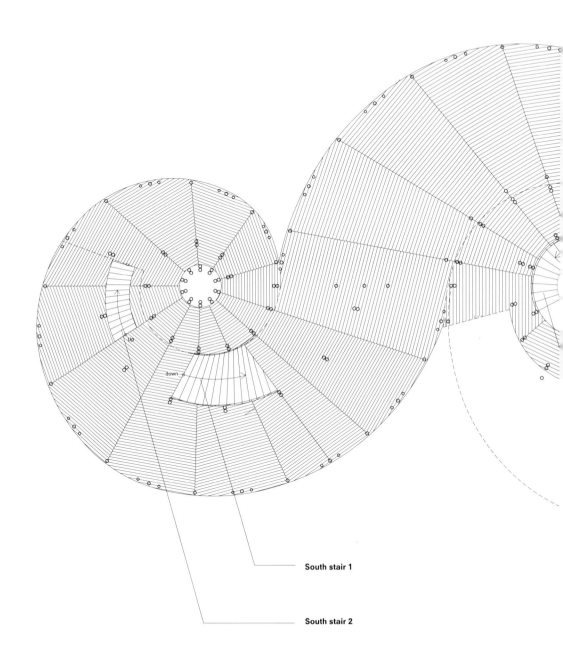

South stair 1

South stair 2

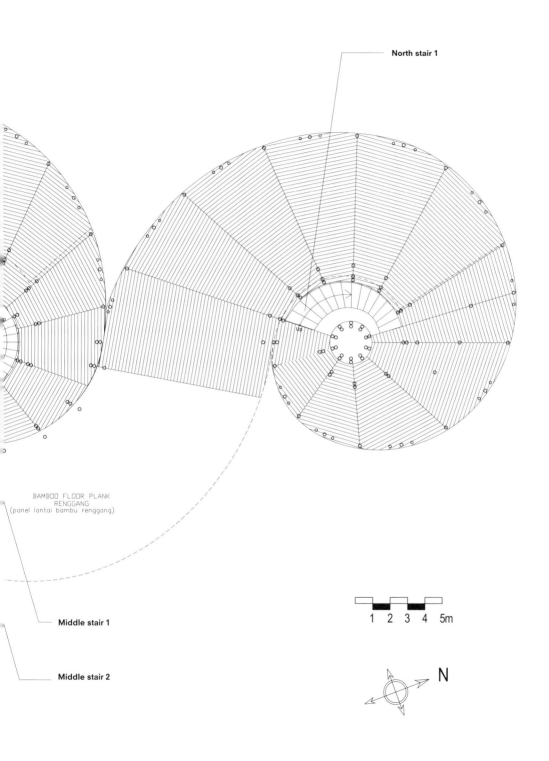

First floorplan

Chandgaon Mosque
Chittagong, Bangladesh

The Chandgaon Mosque is located in Chandgaon village on the northern periphery of Chittagong, Bangladesh's second-largest city. Home to the country's largest port, the sprawling city of 2.5 million is a crowded South Asian metropolis with little meaningful public space or architecture as a result of rapid urbanisation and industrialisation beginning in the late 1980s. Chandgaon village, with 4,500 inhabitants, is quickly undergoing change due to the growing ready-made garments sector. Rice paddies dominate the village landscape, but the pressures of real estate speculation and garment factory expansion are transforming the area.

The large Chandgaon Mosque sits next to an older mosque in the middle of the village's changing dynamics, with its monolithic, spare geometric clarity making a definitive architectural statement towards the contemporary. After a series of turns on a narrow tree-lined dirt road, the Chandgaon Mosque appears, its white exterior and clean geometries in distinct contrast to the natural setting. Despite its scale, the building is at the same height as the dense green foliage and does not overpower its surroundings. The perimeter wall provides a buffer on one side, while a cluster of bamboo taller than the Mosque leans over its roof to frame the composition. The visual and formal strategy of contrasting the regularity of the Mosque's simple forms with the texture, colour and density of its surroundings is followed throughout the project.

The two main spaces of the Chandgaon Mosque, a closed main space and a series of open courts, reflect the traditional organisational typology of Bangladesh mosque architecture. The simplification of religious functions are increased in scale, highlighted through space and light, to create a sense of presence that connects the religious and spiritual to the surrounding flora and sky. The shaping volumes and walls that organise space and light are exemplified most dramatically in the wide oculus above the forecourt. As one enters beneath the compressed horizontal arched opening to the vertical space under the circular oculus, light drops down into the space, with no trees or other buildings visible, connecting this forecourt space directly to the sky.

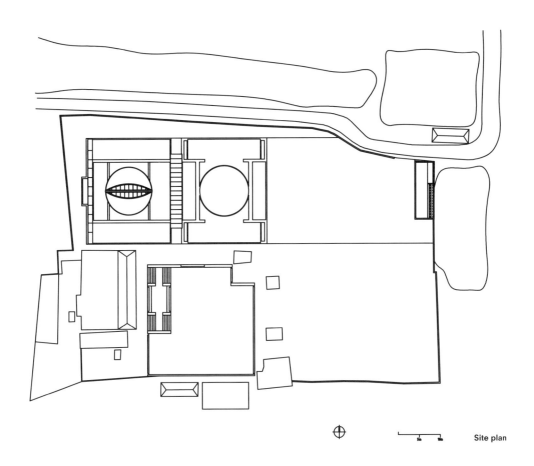

Site plan

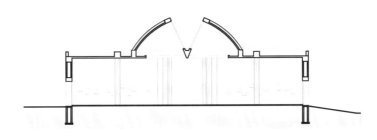

Section B-B

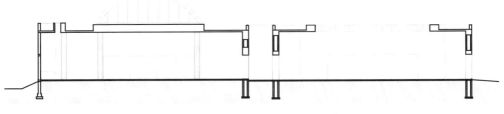

Section A-A

Nishorgo Oirabot Nature Interpretation Centre
Teknaf, Bangladesh

The Nishorgo Oirabot Nature Interpretation Centre is an ecotourism visitor centre located in the Teknaf Game Reserve forests, a protected area outside the town of Teknaf in southern Bangladesh on the banks of the Naf River. Teknaf is located in the Cox's Bazar District, home to one of the world's longest natural sea beaches, and is a major fishing port. From the early Buddhist civilisation up through British rule, this area has been the site of many different cultures, languages and religions. After a period of shipping industrialisation in the 1970s, Cox's Bazar is now undergoing rapid change as a resort area, with the construction of hotels and condominiums in a booming speculative real estate market catering to national Bangladeshi tourism. "Nishorgo", meaning "the natural environment in which people live" in Bengali, is a social programme initiated in 2004 by the Bangladesh Forest Department as a comprehensive effort to preserve the unique beauty and biodiversity of tropical forests through a government partnership with local residents, including resource co-management and economic assistance.

    The Centre's design concept originated from the architects' research of the dominant vernacular house types in this hilly region. The two-storey structure consists of two slabs supported on three load-bearing shear walls and two columns. Each shear wall and column has individual footings below grade connected by grade beams, and the entrance ramp is supported by two separate columns. Despite the use of reinforced concrete, the building's thin slabs and extended cantilevers at the veranda and entrance ramp retain the lightness of local timber architecture through highly formal yet simple gestures. The first-floor space seems to float as the horizontal structural elements are visually lost in the trees. The building is sited on a north-south axis, with the veranda facing the southwest wind and east toward the Naf River. Sensitivity to trees dictated that holes would be "punched" in the roof slab, and the surrounding topography was unaffected by the construction. The building advances architecture into a new direction in Bangladesh through a process-oriented abstract understanding of the vernacular's ecological and climatic capabilities elegantly mapped onto a new architectonic condition.

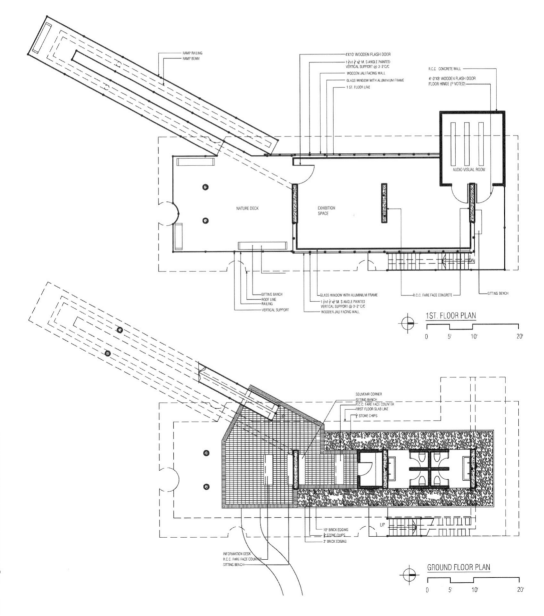

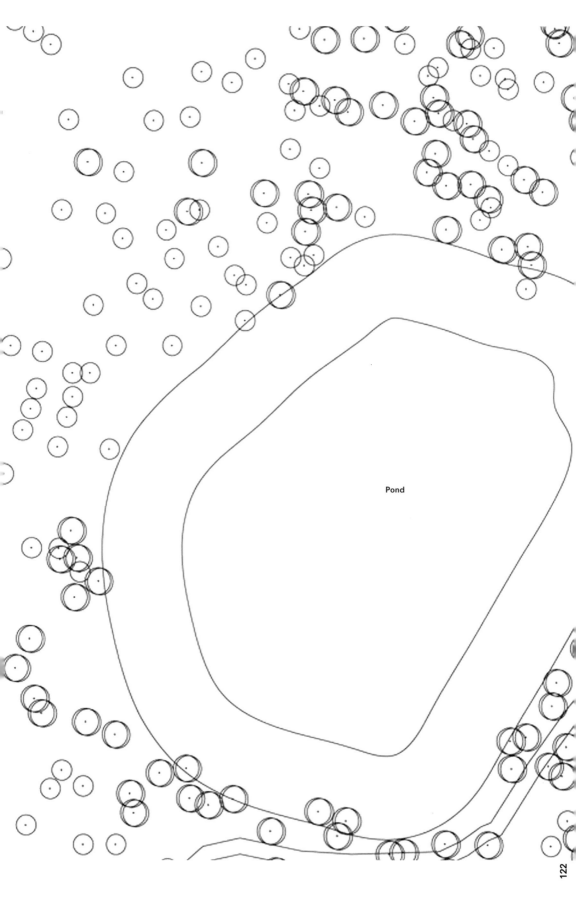

Plane field

Site plan

Industry

The productivity of a society is highly dependent on the opportunities afforded by its places of work. The Ipekyol Textile Factory in Edirne, Turkey, and the Rubber Smokehouse in Kedah, Malaysia, are two very different examples of this type of building. The first is a large new construction, the second a small restoration project. The environments and conditions of such places directly affect the well-being of the workers and the quality of their work. These examples reveal the importance of design even when applied to buildings that have historically been considered merely functional and practical.

Ipekyol Textile Factory
Edirne, Turkey

In the second half of the 20th century, Turkey witnessed a rise in industrial production due to low labour costs, improved machine technology and better transportation connectivity. As a result, industrial factories appeared on the edge of most major cities. The Ipekyol Factory aims to depart from the precedent of generic factories scattered between Istanbul and the site, most of which are metal-clad or precast concrete single-storey sheds that have a neglected aspect and little to no relation to their contexts.

The Ipekyol Factory is located in the City of Edirne, which borders Greece and Bulgaria, with easily accessibility from Istanbul. Edirne has a rich historical heritage given its location between European and Asian Anatolia, including the walls and towers from Edirne Castle, built by the Roman emperor Hadrian, the famous Selimiye Mosque from the Ottoman Period and the recently restored Sultan Bayezid II, with its hospital dating back to 1484. The city has a population of 120,000, including many skilled fabric workers.

Before building the factory, the client realised that to address changes in local and international consumer patterns, he would need to improve product quality. He also knew that he needed to invest in new digital manufacturing technologies, so he toured the globe and developed a process line to combine the most advanced machinery with local systems. He wanted to put procedures and systems in place that assured the highest quality. From this he determined how many machines would be required and their necessary spatial relationships; a preliminary design for the factory's working spaces provided a broad idea of the floor space needed for the new building and its circulation. He recognised the importance of design, even for a building used mostly for production and distribution. He believed in Ipekyol's responsibility towards its employees and understood that the architecture of his workplace would have a substantial influence on the image of the company and its products.

The site has a north-south depth of approximately 300 metres, but only a 130 metres east-west width. To the west is a five-storey technical college building and playground constructed 20 years ago. The eastern boundary is a field with an abandoned development near the highway. The building is 150 x 100 metres in plan, and 14 metres high, containing production facilities, a training school, and administration and catering areas. A surface car park, a play area, and a plant room are located outside.

The plant is organised with structural grids and five internal gardens of various sizes that create a safe, legible environment and encourage communication between different parts of the production system. The even distribution of columns encourages manageable foundation loads, allowing the use of simple strip and pad foundations to optimise the site's cut and fill balance. On top of the columns sits a grid of traditional steel roof trusses approximately 2.5 metres deep, and a secondary purlins and metal cladding system then sits over the trusses to support the roof insulation and membrane. Cross bracing and vertical bracing systems provide structural stability.

The single volume gives a clear sense of community, blurring the hierarchy between administration staff, maintenance staff, students and factory workers. The U-shaped system flows efficiently through production, packaging and dispatch of each garment, and controls for error with a robust quality-assurance system. All wall finishes are exposed and lightly coloured to take advantage of the transparency of the building, and the material selection and rigorous detailing has taken due consideration of durability and longevity. The increased height of the building and internal courtyards maximises daylight and thermal performance, reduces energy use and encourages natural ventilation. The innovation lies in the rigour, detailing and quality of the final construction.

One of the factory's strongest features is a water pool that runs along the full length of the southern glazed wall, which provides some cooling effect through evaporation during the summer and calmly welcomes visitors with its reflection on the wall. The water-collection system moves rainfall from the large roof and discharges into concealed drainage channels around the edges of the building. The pool has considerable capacity to absorb storm-water runoff, and the gardens are also treated with controlled drainage systems to prevent flooding.

Jury Citation

The intelligent and imaginative design and engineering of the Ipekyol Textile Factory make it a role model of an efficient and pleasant working environment for any industry, and exceptionally so for the textile industry where such qualities are rare.

The building combines functional efficiency with humanity to the commercial advantage of the client. Made mostly from local materials, it sits lightly on its plot. The high ceilings and internal courtyards maximise the flow of daylight and encourage natural ventilation, making the work spaces more agreeable as well as reducing energy usage and improving thermal performance. Water is collected from the roof and drained into the local system, but may eventually be recycled for use by the factory. Production and administration are housed within the same building, and are visible to each other, improving internal communications and fostering team spirit.

At a time when the Muslim world is industrialising rapidly, and many countries, including Turkey, need to develop higher-quality products to counter rising labour costs, the Ipekyol Textile Factory demonstrates how enlightened design can create a replicable blueprint of a cleaner, safer, more efficient workplace that can also achieve higher productivity and profitability.

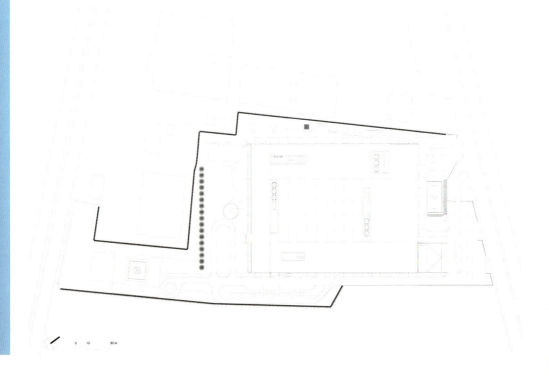

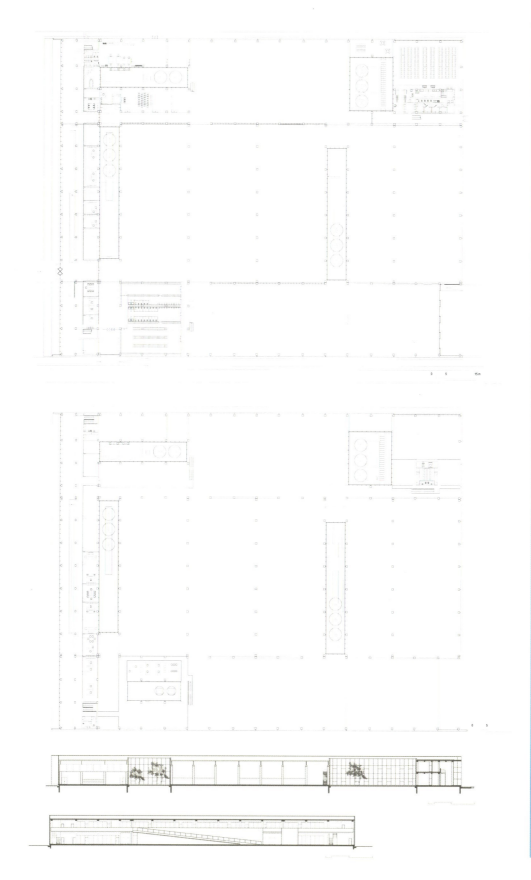

Restoration of Rubber Smokehouse
Kedah, Malaysia

Lunas is a two-road township situated in the Kedah district on mainland Malaysia, with Chinese, Indian and Malay populations. The town was established at the end of the 19th century to service the rubber plantations, and its history reflects Malaysia's broader history of colonialism, plantations and migrant populations. While modern industrial technology allows natural rubber to ship to factories as latex jelly, it originally had to be rolled into rubber sheets and smoked to preserve its characteristics. As a cash crop, rubber ceased to be the backbone of Malaysia's economy in the late 1970s, when its global price fell with the introduction of synthetic rubber. Lunas's economic decline was reflected in its physical circumstance, as was the case for many small towns throughout the country. The Lunas Rubber Smokehouse stands as an example of Malaysia's industrial heritage and the rubber industry that was of vital importance to the country's economy for much of the 20th century.

Until recently, this history had gone unnoticed. But in 2005, DiGi Telecommunication launched a program to celebrate Malaysia's diverse heritage. They asked the public to nominate five "Amazing Malaysians" who have made a special contribution to cultural heritage, and Kedah's Heritage Architect Laurence Loh was nominated. Loh was asked to propose a project with the condition that it involve schoolchildren working alongside him, and he chose the smokehouse. The project converted the smokehouse into an interpretation centre and museum, with a permanent exhibition showcasing the rubber-planting past, along with Lunas's architectural and urban history.

The project identified Chinese, Indian and Malay schoolchildren between the ages of 10 and 15 from three ethnically segregated local schools, who participated in cultural mapping and videography trainings every weekend for three months. The project sought to teach the children true intercultural and inter-religious tolerance, and how to document and interpret their cultural inheritance by gathering oral histories of the town.

The merit of the project lies in its unique approach, demonstrating how precise architectural interventions can help to restore a neglected heritage and play a role in advancing social cohesion in multicultural societies.

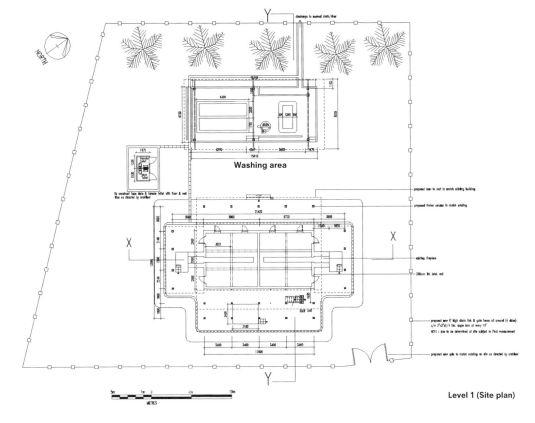

Level 1 (Site plan)

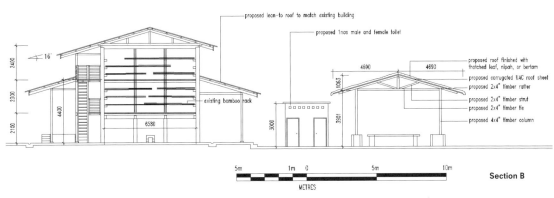

Section B

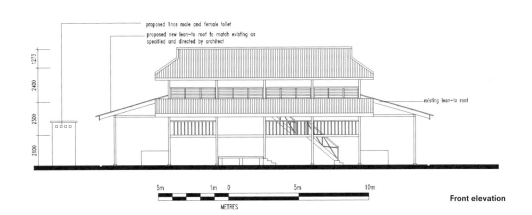

Front elevation

Dwelling

From houses to housing, domestic architecture inscribes the pattern and quality of our daily lives. The Tulou Collective Housing in Guangzhou, China, and the Palmyra House in Alibagh, India, represent the two scales of domestic architecture. The first is a large circular and monumental building on the outskirts of a city with 20 million inhabitants. It gives order and identity to its nondescript surroundings. The second is a modest retreat composed of two double-storey timber buildings that demonstrate genuine sensitivity in the choice of materials and location, and in understanding climate conditions. Together with other selected projects, these buildings and their interiors are material manifestations of our lifestyle choices and preferences. How should we live alone, and how should we live with others?

Tulou Collective Housing
Guangzhou, China

Nanhai District is part of greater Guangzhou, the third-largest city in China, with an estimated population of 20 million. In the late 1970s, Guangzhou's economy developed thriving businesses and manufacturing sectors, and attracted migrant workers from throughout the country. Today Guangzhou continues to urbanise rapidly, with crisscrossing expressways and high-rise housing blocks dominating the landscape. On the periphery, agricultural land is converted for residential use, with farmers building apartment structures on their land. In this environment, the Tulou Collective Housing project is a welcome change.

Tulou Collective Housing, known also as Urban Tulou, is a low-rise apartment block for low-income groups, many of whom are migrant workers. The project's client saw the traditional, circular, multifamily *tulou* houses in the rural Fujian province and wanted to explore the possibility of a modern urban interpretation. A piece of land was available at a Guangzhou project that was not suitable for higher-income housing because it was located next to a highway. Government regulations require that a certain percentage of units in large-scale housing developments include lower-rent units, and this provided the opportunity for a low-income housing typology experiment.

The shape of the block is inspired by the *tulou*: extended families' housing units were along the periphery, lower floors had no openings, upper-level openings were very small and the central space was for community activities. Unlike modern urban housing structures, the *tulou* form offered the opportunity to introduce shared community spaces within its introverted shape. The project consists of an outer circular block, with an interior rectangular block connected to the outer ring by bridges, and an inner courtyard. Both blocks contain 287 apartment units, and the interstitial spaces are for circulation and community use.

The architects explored minimum spatial standards, and in consultation with finance personnel they developed a functional program of 40-square-metre apartments, each with two bedrooms, cooking facilities, a dining/living space, and a toilet. Open community spaces evolved during the form's development. The Urban Tulou is a unique experiment in low-income housing that has replication potential as an affordable, comfortable and appropriate urban form.

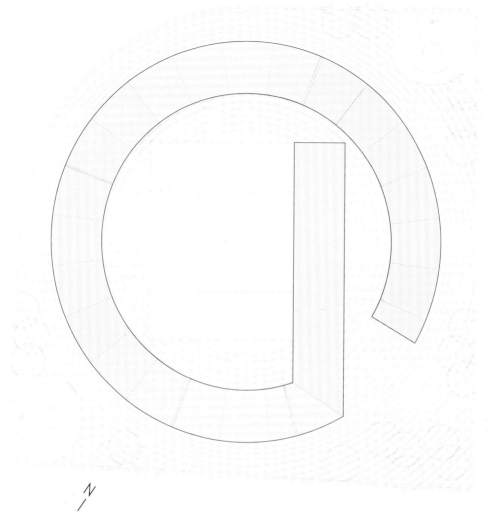

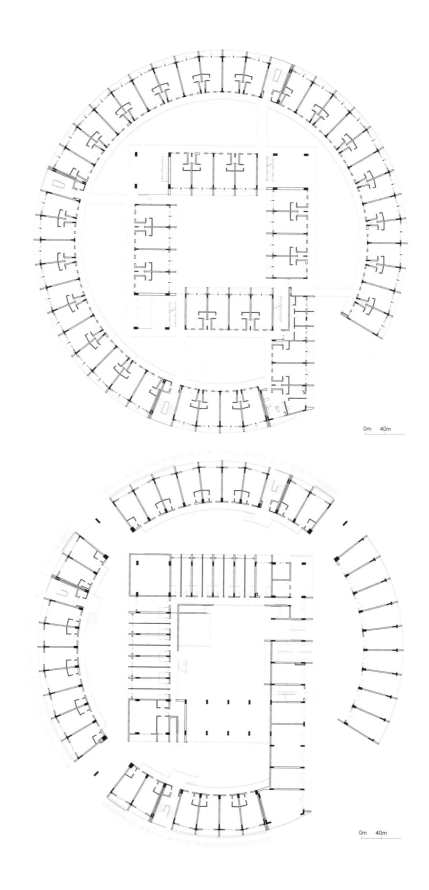

Palmyra House
Alibagh, India

Located two hours from Mumbai, near the fishing town of Nandgaon, the Palmyra House is a double-storey weekend retreat house. The programme was organised in two parallel oblong, louvered masses, with a central pool serving as the uniting space that extends westward to the sea. The site is located on an agricultural parcel under coconut trees, principally for screened views of the sea and their passive, shaded cooling throughout the day. A minimal number of trees were removed, despite obvious dangers of falling coconuts and the heavy fronds, such that attentive maintenance is required for the grove.

Intimately detailed and constructed, the structural system employs post-and-lintel timber for all vertical loading. The block elevations feature louvers made from the trunks of the local palmyra palm *(Borassus flabellifer)*, an indigenous agricultural crop cultivated for its nutritious fruit and the highly valued durable wood. There is no decoration on the block elevations, and the exposed construction details contribute to the overall texture of the building. With minimal enclosure, the house puts occupants in intimate contact with air flow, humidity, temperature, sound and smell. Apart from the adjustable teak louver doors, the enclosure is a permeable skin of palmyra wood louvers gently angled downward from inside to outside.

The landscape design for the project was conceived around the coconut grove, both formally and functionally. At the main gate to the property, a betel nut palm forest was added to the existing grove as a buffer to a neighbouring house. The dirt driveway terminates immediately after the gate, giving way to a narrow footpath along the side of the north property wall, which the architect softens by topping it with aqueduct channels, acknowledging the many lower masonry aqueducts in the region. The path broadens as it nears the house obliquely, with the forest ending as the sparser trunks of the coconut grove take over. With the oblique entry, the angled north face of the master bedroom wing comes into view first, and the cantilevered box of the master bath hangs lightly over the brown sand below.

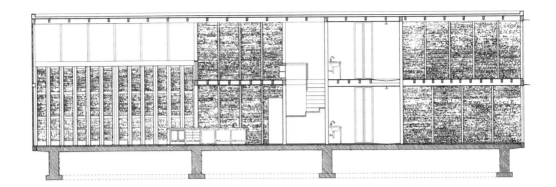

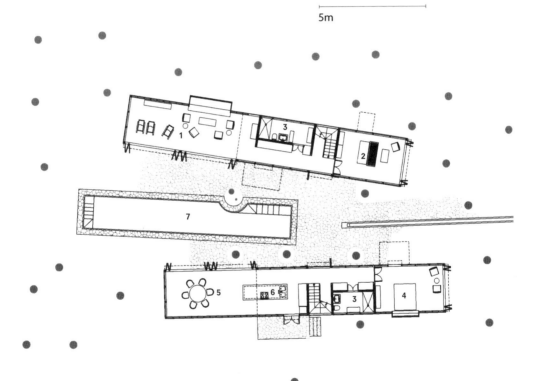

1 Living room
2 Study
3 Bathroom
4 Bedroom
5 Dining
6 Kitchen
7 Pool

Dowlat II Residential Building
Tehran, Iran

Tehran is situated on the slope of the Alborz Mountains, with a population of 7 million people. The Dowlat II project's northern neighbourhood is among Tehran's oldest, and originally had a series of gardens owned by affluent families. Over the last decade, small developers have identified the area as a promising investment zone, and the district's small lots have been developed into four- and five-storey middle-class apartments.

Tehran has a history of speculative housing development. Well-connected developers generated great wealth by sidestepping planning and architectural processes, opting for mass-produced housing typologies that damaged the quality of the city's built environment. With clear profit motivations, investor guidelines are simple: maximise the inhabitable surface area while minimising the square-footage cost. Once the spatial organisation of structural columns is set, based on per unit municipal parking requirements, facade opacity is reserved for areas that coincide with the structural elements, and transparency for what is left, such that aesthetic challenges are generally reduced to two-dimensional choices for envelope design.

To avoid mere cosmetic design, Arsh Design Studio treated the Dowlat II facade as a "micro-section" or "wall section"—a point of view perpendicular to the conventional frontal view—to be developed three-dimensionally. The small residential building has four separate apartments, and its facade is comprised of a two-tier system: the interior tier seals the inhabitable spaces from environmental factors, and the exterior tier consists of a wooden grid punctuated with a variety of kinetic openings, extending the building's volume beyond its main envelope and generating a multiplicity of compositions. The building is not only responsive to its users but adds a sense of excitement to the public streetscape it overlooks. The project was popularly elected as the most likable facade in the city and has been replicated by the architect and others.

Sectional variation further allows for creative spatial qualities while building to maximum allowed square footage. Dowlat II's sectional disposition provides access of the upper unit to a private roof garden and multiple unit designs within the same building, which is not common in Tehran's prototypical floor plans.

1 Entrance
2 Living room
3 Dining room
4 WC
5 Kitchen
6 Bedroom
7 Bath room
8 Sitting room
9 Void
10 Roof garden
11 Parking

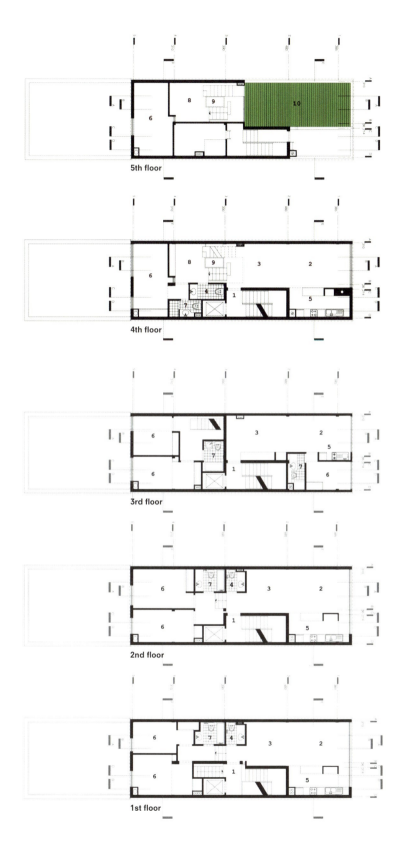

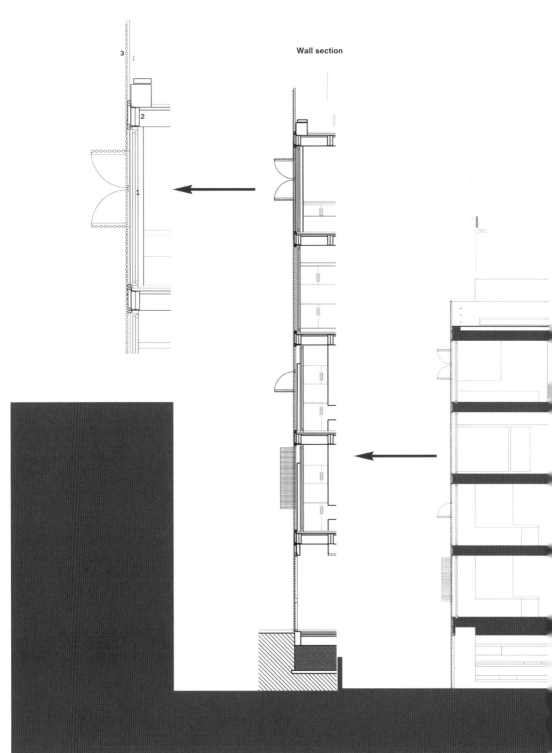

Wall section

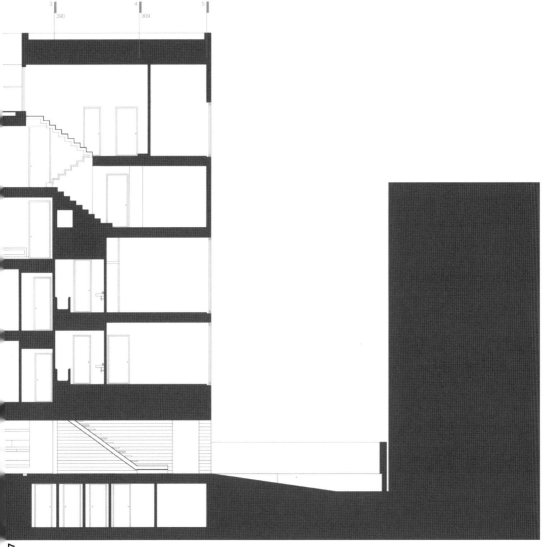

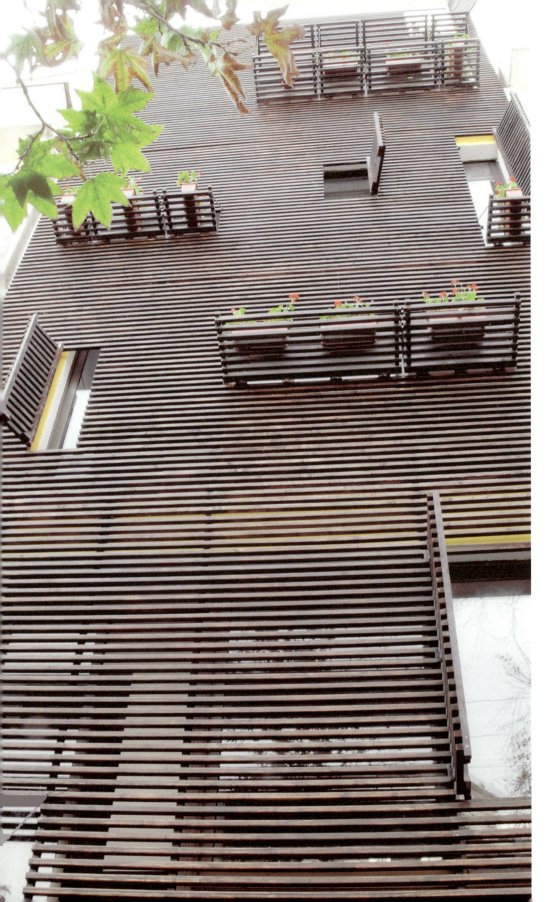

Yodakandyia Community Centre
Hambantota District, Sri Lanka

A 2004 tsunami devastated great swathes of Sri Lanka along the southeastern coastline: 35,300 people lost their lives, 21,400 were injured and 516,000 became displaced. In the aftermath, the government established a 300-metre environmental buffer zone along the sea, which meant that hundreds of families could not return to rebuild their homes. The government then designated Tissamaharama in the interior southeast as part of an expanded settlement programme to accommodate 218 displaced families from coastal areas.

In 2005, UN Habitat organised Tissamaharama's displaced communities for the Yodakandyia housing reconstruction project, located several kilometres outside of town. The communities formed Community Development Councils (CDCs) and supplied the labour for the project, and the government provided the land. Once the houses were completed, local authorities gave property deeds to the families. The CDCs then formed the Pinsara Federation and drew up the initial brief for a community centre. The centre was located in the heart of Yodakandyia and included a preschool, a library and IT centre, a clinic and a cricket field and volleyball court. The federation invited Architecture for Humanity to join UN Habitat as technical advisors for the centre's design and construction. A series of community action planning meetings helped transform their initial vision into a workable design. The three structures fitted in well with the surrounding small houses, and the arrangement helped avoid excessive heat build-up.

Clay tiles covered the timber on a steeply pitched roof to ensure efficient water shedding during monsoon seasons. The angle of pitch was then reduced at the edges by sprocketed eaves to slow the rainwater and collect it in guttering, where it was channeled to storage tanks for reuse. The bricks were locally handmade, which helped avoid the steep rise in construction material costs after the tsunami. Certain bricks were omitted in the laying sequence, forming small openings known as *jalis* that allow daylight into the building without the cost of a window.

The Yodakandyia Community Centre was the result of efforts to invest in a common spirit and build a self-sustaining community from a vulnerable, diverse group of families affected by the tsunami.

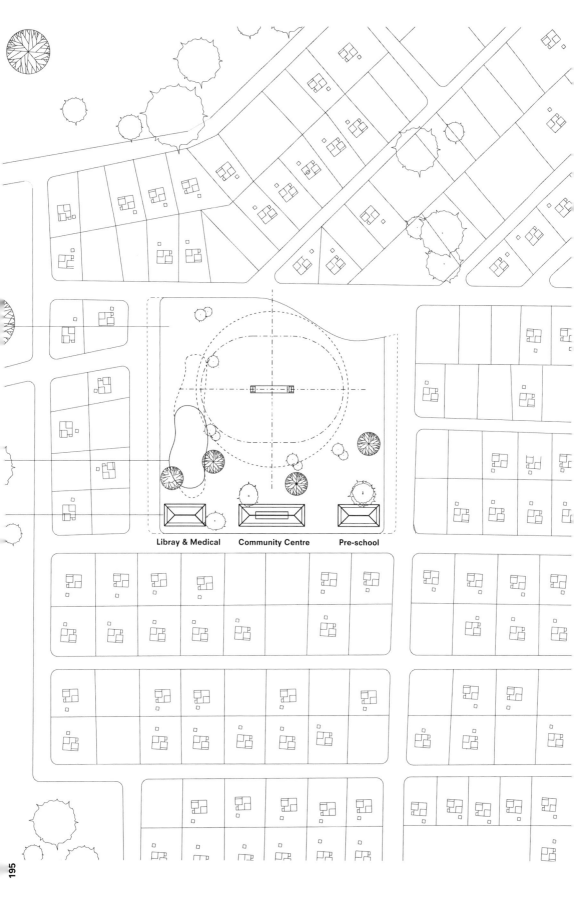

Reconstruction of Ngibikan Village
Yogyakarta, Indonesia

The village of Ngibikan is situated in the Bantul Province, south of Yogyakarta, on the island of Java. In the immediate surrounding area, every inch of land is used for either farming or small housing settlements. Contained cultivated fields dominate this rural landscape, but the region is still one of the most densely populated areas in Indonesia with 1,600 people per square kilometre. Java is located on the boundary of three major tectonic plates—the Indo-Australian Plate, the Eurasian Plate and the Filipino Plate—in a region prone to volcanoes, earthquakes and tsunamis.

On 27 May 2006, an earthquake hit Indonesia, and its epicentre was less than 10 kilometres from Ngibikan. The village was destroyed, killing more than 5,700 people and severely damaging more than 140,000 homes in the region. Immediately following the earthquake, the popular *Kompas* newspaper called Eko Prawoto, a renowned local architect, to ask how they could help with rebuilding. The newspaper collected donations from its readers and financed the reconstruction of one of the village neighbourhoods, or *Rukun Tetangga* (RT). RT No. 5 consisted of 55 families, or approximately 250 individuals, and with design input from Prawoto and their community leader Maryono, the villagers reconstructed 65 homes in less than 90 days.

The rebuilt village of Ngibikan sits on the footprint of the existing village, and the new homes are based on a vernacular building type, the *limasan* house, with innovative modifications to ensure resistance from future earthquakes. The traditional *limasan* homes responded directly to the equatorial climate, including a flexible interior layout with no interior walls and no permanent partitions. This flexibility allowed a variety of uses, responding to the agricultural cycle, changing family needs and social activities. While the iconic roofline is retained, the innovations and adjustments include concrete columns to elevate the wooden frames from the ground, fibre cement board for exterior cladding, and a new structural frame of wooden trusses, with metal bolts for resistance in tension and compression. Recycled doors, windows and decorative motifs were also added by villagers to make each house an expression of their own personality.

Block before earthquake

Block plan after reconstruction

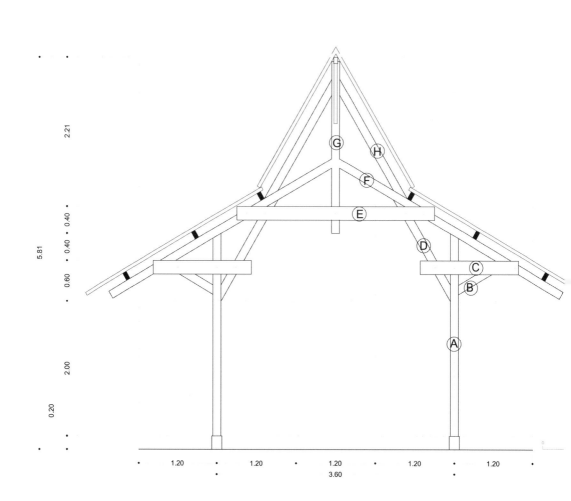

Conservation

How can we make the best examples of our architectural, landscape and urban heritage endure over time? Critical and strategic approaches to conservation have the capacity to make these exemplars adapt to new circumstances and new uses. From the Revitalisation of the Hypercentre of Tunis, Tunisia, to the Conservation of Gjirokastra, Albania, urban areas previously facing decay and disintegration have been rebuilt and renovated to provide dynamic public spaces, institutions and commercial districts. Strategic conservation and adaptive reuse make buildings and cities sustainable catalysts for alternative forms of economic and cultural development.

Revitalisation of the Hypercentre of Tunis
Tunis, Tunisia

Tunis is a Mediterranean city that underwent major urban transformations in the late 19th century as a French Protectorate. A new layout, adjacent to the medina, formed the body of the Ville Nouvelle, also known as the Hypercentre or Bab B'Har (meaning "the sea gate" in Arabic). The Ville Nouvelle was built on the eastern side of the medina, while the southern, northern and western surroundings consisted of fortifications, cemeteries and olive fields. Governed by France's first *règlement de voirie*, the rational, ordered grid plan changed the medina's historic walled urban pattern, as well as the city's character, by emphasising priorities of hygiene and commerce. The new town was planned around the strategic Avenue de la Marine (named Habib Bourguiba after independence in 1956), often referred to as Champs Élysées de Tunis. New monuments were added to its established cultural structures, including two theatres, the Rossini Palace and the Municipal Theatre. These urban transformations created spaces for important cultural encounters between the city's native and colonial heritage.

Tunis has taken an unprecedented step towards the conservation of its colonial heritage, which is often destroyed in other North African countries because it evokes memories of colonisation. However, this more recent heritage is worthy of consideration as a vehicle for important artistic, architectural and urban exchange between the north and south of the Mediterranean. The revitalisation of this heritage is essential to improve the urban environment and to preserve the memory of complex North African cities. Tunis's pioneering step in considering all types of architecture, whether native or colonial, as heritage occurred thanks to the efforts of the Association de Sauvegarde de la Médina de Tunis (ASM) in making officials and the public aware of heritage matters, particularly after its success, since 1980, in conserving the Tunis medina. As a result, the necessity of including 19th- and 20th-century heritage in preservation plans became an increasing preoccupation of specialists and politicians alike. The revitalisation project has proven the potential of such colonial heritage as a cultural, touristic and economic asset for the city.

In 1988, the Tunisian government launched an initiative for the classification of historic monuments that were visibly dilapidated. The result included five public buildings of major importance in the modern urban history of Tunis, the first to be considered historic monuments since independence. Following this growing concern, ASM launched a project entitled Projet d'Embellissement de l'Hypercentre de Tunis using a holistic approach to identify the dysfunctions of this sensitive, high-value, recent heritage area.

With a limited budget, the pioneering urban approach to addressing architectural issues was developed to intervene in key monuments as well as to undertake an urban upgrading for the Hypercentre's public space. The project consisted of an urban revitalisation plan to restructure 60,000 square metres of public spaces and make them chiefly pedestrian. Key dilapidated monuments and facades for approximately 130 decayed buildings were rehabilitated following leading architectural and urban technical guidelines. Public squares were given priority as nodal points that enhance the urban experience, and the Place de la Victoire and Place du 7 Novembre, in particular, were meticulously reorganised and renovated. To enhance nightlife, ASM restored and redesigned all public lighting around the site of the project, which increased security tremendously, as well as the area's public use. To articulate all of these actions, ASM studied its entire landscape and redesigned it as a continuous and rhythmic walking experience with improved street furniture and green spaces. The landscape design created more shade during summertime, enhanced the visibility of urban facades and recovered open vistas on both sides of the avenue, and created a balance between vehicular and pedestrian circuits.

The projects were carried out through the meticulous and dexterous rehabilitation work of mainly local craftsmen. Local architects were also very involved in the process and supervised the rehabilitation work. The ASM brought some of these rehabilitation skills from its restoration work on Tunis's medina, but new skills were also gained, including the decorative paintings on the theatre ceilings by local artists and painters. In addition to the successful functional programme, the revitalisation project of recent heritage has increased the area's real estate value as well as the levels of business in downtown Tunis.

Jury Citation

The revitalisation of the late-nineteenth and early-twentieth century built heritage in the Hypercentre district—Bab B'Har—of Tunis, is an important and inspiring contribution to our changing understanding of the recent history of the Islamic world, particularly of the cultural legacy of the colonial era.

The achievement of the Association de Sauvegarde de la Médina de Tunis (ASM) lies in preserving the important landmarks and facades of this period, which have been neglected and destroyed in many Muslim cities, and using them as the catalyst for an ambitious and eclectic economic regeneration programme. The project has not only created a lively and prosperous area, but fostered a richer, more nuanced understanding of Tunisia's recent history, without disguising the nature of colonialism.

Equally impressive is the process through which the ASM, a tiny, passionately committed organisation of modest means, transferred the technical knowledge gained in their earlier preservation of the old medina to the Hypercentre. The local community was consulted throughout to ensure that existing businesses would benefit from regeneration, and that the process would be sustainable. These goals were reflected in the innovative financing of the project, and in the training oflocal craftsmen to undertake the restoration work.

During the colonial era, many Muslim countries were the focus of modernist experimentation, often by young European architects developing radical ideas. The sensitivity and ambition of the revitalisation of the Hypercentre in Tunis shows how the same Muslim countries can now play an equally innovative and influential role in the preservation of modern heritage.

215 Aga Khan Award for Architecture

Souk Waqif
Doha, Qatar

Souk Waqif is a local market in Doha that played a major role in the city's development. Located on the banks of Wadi Mishrieb River, Souk Waqif's name ("Standing Market" in Arabic) was derived from merchants selling their goods while standing when its banks were wet during wintertime. The urban layout is not as complex as other souks in the Muslim world, as the pattern was constructed through more spontaneous and gradual processes. The souk covers a 164,000-square-metre area and is organised in three parts: large storage areas for wholesale and retail, craft shops, and open-air stalls.

In 2000, the Emir of Qatar, His Highness Sheikh Hamad bin Khalifa al Thani, invited international experts to propose a design for the reconstruction of the souk, but he was not pleased with the results. The Emir then asked the Qatari artist Mohamed Ali Abdullah to provide him with his vision of the souk's reconstruction. Exploring remaining dilapidated structures of an overused souk, the artist was able to rejuvenate the memory of the place through artistic mediums and field research. The artist presented several watercolour drawings, and the Emir ordered work to start immediately.

The souk provides a long walking itinerary, animated with quality restaurants and coffee shops. It is the only open-air public shopping space in Doha. All buildings have the same structural system: a skeleton constituted of a series of pillars in sun-baked bricks supporting light beams of "dangeel" wood. The roofs are made of bamboo covered with matting and a layer of clay that serves as a stabiliser and a ground for the upper floors. The materials act as an efficient means of insulation between inside and outside, which optimises the use of energy.

Educational materials are displayed throughout to remind the passerby of the memory of the souk. All services are within walking distance, and the vehicular circulation is managed outside the pedestrian zones. In contrast to heritage theme parks known throughout Gulf cities, the Souk Waqif is a unique architectural revival of one of Doha's most important heritage sites, where the designer succeeds in creating an authentic and original experience.

Conservation of Gjirokastra
Gjirokastra, Albania

Gjirokastra is located at the centre of an emerging cultural tourism sector in southern Albania. Gjirokastra is a well-preserved example of an Ottoman Balkan town, with an enormous castle rising above it. The town has a Greco-Roman past and is surrounded by the natural and archaeological resources of the Drino Valley.

The Ottomans conquered Albania in the early 15th century and Gjirokastra, with its strategic location and rich agricultural hinterland, was made a provincial capital. In the following centuries, residential districts expanded and lavish houses were built in an Ottoman idiom, incorporating local features and materials. Enver Hoxha, dictator of communist Albania for four decades after World War II, was a native of Gjirokastra, and in 1960 he declared his hometown a "museum city". Seven years later, he established an Institute of Monuments (IoM), and although it could not save religious buildings, the IoM classified the town's heritage and restored many of its buildings. In 1992 both the regime and the economy collapsed, and the town's institutional structure disintegrated. Many of its skilled craftsmen emigrated to Greece, and in 1997, anti-government violence destroyed much of the city's bazaar.

The idea of heritage and architectural conservation is at least 50 years old in Gjirokastra, so the contemporary challenge is that of rebuilding capacity and making conservation relevant to a changed society and economy.

This is the historical context for the work of the Gjirokastra Conservation and Development Organization (GCDO). Since 2001, GCDO has endeavoured to save the town's decaying heritage and to focus on the development potential of conservation, emphasising human as well as built resources. With its partner institutions and a growing pool of donors, GCDO's grassroots work includes: the restoration of two notable houses, restoration of the fountains and square of a 17th-century bathhouse, building stabilisation, the rehabilitation of the bazaar and restoration of the castle, which will soon house a museum devoted to the town's history and architecture. Restoration projects are now designed with an eye to reuse and sustainability, integrating training, business development and community outreach. Two such projects are the Artisan Incubator and the training of young restoration architects.

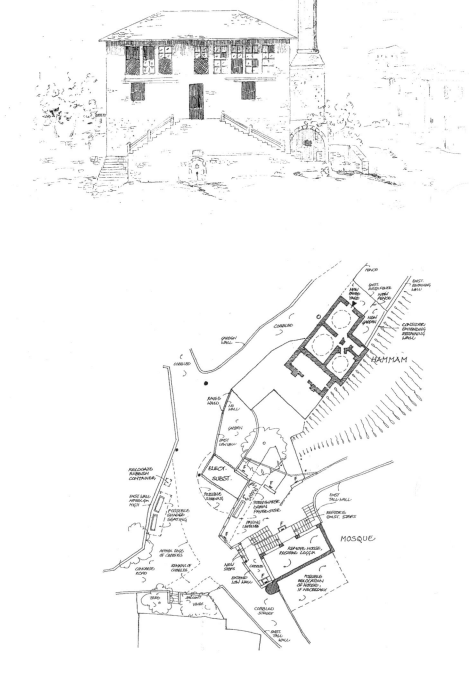

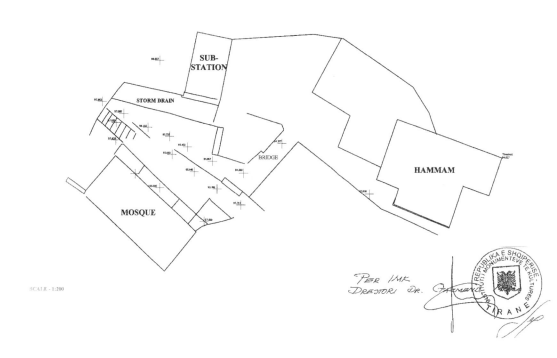

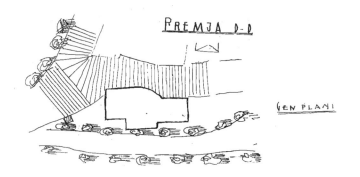

HAMAMI MEÇITES

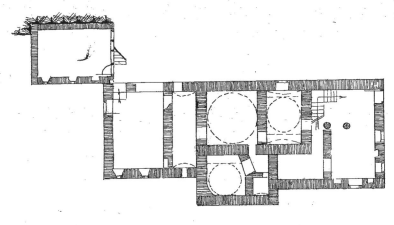

KATI I

PER IMK
DREJTORI DR. GAZMEND MUKA

HAMAMI MEÇITES

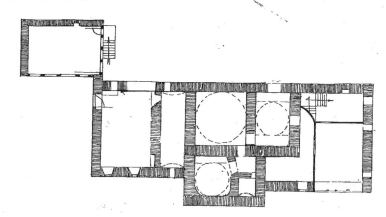

KATI II-te.

PER IMK
DREJTORI DR. GAZMEND MUKA

Rehabilitation of Al-Karaouine Mosque
Fez, Morocco

The Karaouine Mosque is located at the heart of the Fez Medina and is an integral part of the city's urban fabric. It is architecturally characteristic of the larger Maghreb region, inspired by the monuments of al-Andalus. Al-Karaouine also hosts a university, considered to be the oldest in the world, which was once a major centre of learning. The ensemble plays a vital role in the spiritual, social and cultural life of the community.

The Karaouine Mosque was built in AD 859 by Fatima Al-Fihriya, whose family was originally from Kairouan, Tunisia, and migrated to Fez at the beginning of the 9th century. It is the first mosque known to have been established by a woman. Fatima's sister, Mariam, built the Andalusian mosque along the eastern bank of the river, and the old city of Fez (Fez al-Bali) developed around the two mosques. The Karaouine Mosque underwent several phases of expansion during subsequent historical periods.

In 2004, King Mohammad VI led prayer at the mosque, and upon noticing its state of deterioration, ordered the immediate restoration of the historic building and its *minbar* (*al-Minbar al-Atiq*). The Ministère des Habous et des Affaires Islamiques supervised the restoration and rehabilitation project. It is possibly the first time in Morocco that a project with such significance and scale completely employed local capacities for research, analyses and execution. An overarching objective of the project was the revival of the cultural and educational role that Al-Karaouine had played in the past.

A measurement of humidity levels found that they had reached a 2-metre height and were especially high during the winter. Humidity had uniformly affected the entire structure and its plaster coating—at full saturation on some pillars, the result of either capillary action from the ground or heavy rainfall. To mitigate the danger, the restoration team implemented two water-drainage systems, both for the court and around the exterior of the mosque. During the restoration work, archaeological remains were discovered, and an emergency programme for the excavation, documentation, study and reburial began immediately.

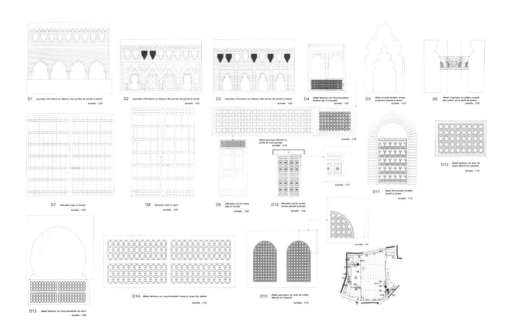

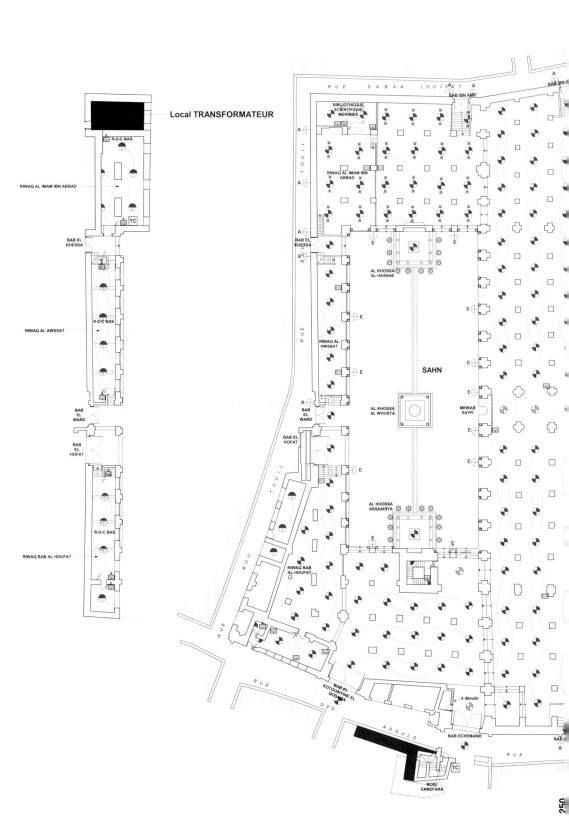

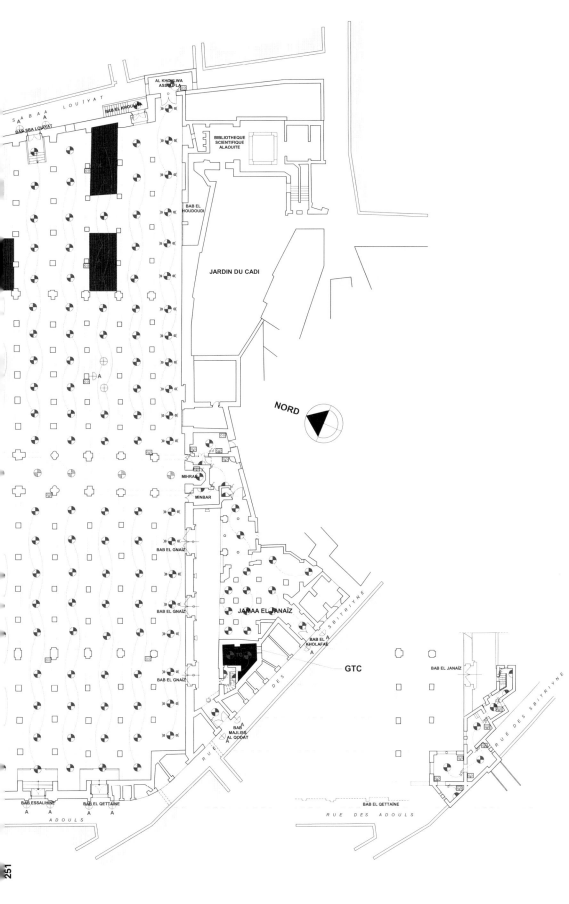

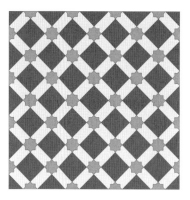

D16 *lemzedej bel ktib et khatem*
(entrée bab el ward)

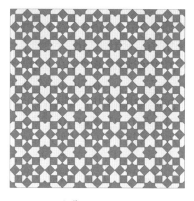

D17 *tarsiã*
(pourtour mur bab el anza)

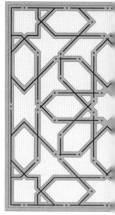

D18 *chemmasia*
(maqsoura)

D19 plâtre sculpté et peint
(pavillon saâdien)

D20 plâtre sculpté et peint
(pavillon saâdien)

D21 rbaoachrini
(pavillon al khassa al hasnaâ)

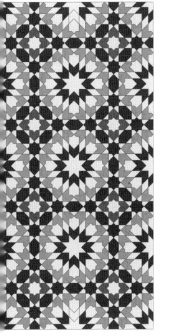

Essays

The Shortlist
Omar Abdulaziz Hallaj

Triannually over the last 30 years, the Aga Khan Award for Architecture has solicited nominations for projects from around the Muslim world that deserve special recognition. The Award receives hundreds of nominations for every cycle, and some 20 to 30 projects are normally shortlisted before the final winners are announced. After the selection of the winning projects, however, the shortlisted project material has been relegated to the archive, accessed only by interested researchers. For this cycle of the Award, a new policy was adopted: The list would be made public. The shortlisted projects would both be honoured by public recognition and contribute to a fuller enunciation of the Award's overall message.

For this cycle, 19 projects were selected for the shortlist. The nominations represent an important spectrum of projects from around the world, exemplifying the diversity and breadth of Muslim presence. Some projects were nominated from traditional Muslim hinterlands; others were identified in places where Muslim communities are a minority—perhaps even a recent addition to societies where Muslims had little presence in the past. This demographic distribution is of course but one small part of the paradigm of defining a Muslim *Ummah*. Diversity in customs, economies and ritual practices all add to the complexity of identifying an overarching cultural ethos that would include all Muslims. It also enriches the possibilities for undertaking such an enterprise.

This time, the Award decided to publish its shortlist partly in response to the need to expand the definition of the Muslim realm and broaden the scope of debate concerning cultural specificity, and partly to address the wide range of innovative solutions available for addressing similar problems. The shortlisted projects reinforce the messages promulgated by the winning projects, but they also enrich these messages by shedding light on the complexity of the built environment. A myriad of technical, economic, social and political concerns are embedded in these projects. The winning projects can epitomise certain values, but can never alone address all issues.

Despite the fact that the shortlist was announced some time before the jury selected the winning projects, there is always a sentiment that a shortlist is secondary. We tend to forget that the issues brought forward by the winning projects come from within the shortlist, and not the other way around. The shortlist is what generates the winning projects; the values of the winning projects were already embodied in the wider selection. The three themes addressed by the winning projects were identified as: the expansion of the presence of Muslim cultures within the framework of globalisation; "treading lightly on earth" as an attitude towards affecting the built environment, regardless of the scale of intervention; and inclusiveness as a strategy for addressing the need to live together in a complex world. These themes are as relevant for the shortlisted projects as they proved to be for the winning projects.

The Tulou Collective Housing complex in Guangzhou, China, is learning from traditional building types found in another part of China; it challenges the very notion of tradition as something indigenous, but manages to redefine a traditional typology to meet modern needs. The Bridge School in northern China is situated between two traditional Tulou structures, yet opts to address its context with a simple modern building. The two projects were not designed with paradigms of Muslim values, but together they reflect an essential theme in Muslim political and cultural discourse today: Is tradition resilient enough to meet the challenges of the modern?

Two projects address post-disaster reconstruction: the post-earthquake rebuilding of Ngibikan village in Indonesia, and the post-tsunami construction of a community centre in Yodakandyia in Sri Lanka to facilitate the integration of refugees from the coastal lowlands into the hinterland. The first invoked an old Muslim value of collaboration to rebuild the village and recycled communal assets to preserve community wealth. The other project reacted to the needs of a non-Muslim community with the same diligence and sensitivity. In the face of disaster, all humans have basic needs and must embrace similar modes of solidarity to recover.

Yet the process of recovery is bigger than any one community can achieve on its own. Perhaps the key issue here is to be always prepared for disaster. Preparedness is now a challenge for all governments and communities across the world. In that context, the Wadi Hanifa Project sheds some light on how governments are taking the initiative to lessen the future dangers of floods and environmental disaster. In the case of Wadi Hanifa, the issue of mitigating environmental disaster is resolved in a way that addresses the very fabric and identity of the city. Genuine responses come from investing in developing a deep understanding of place on all levels and crafting appropriate solutions.

Defining local identity in the face of globalising normative forces was the theme of many projects. Some of the projects addressed the issue in the conservation project format. The Karaouine Mosque in Fez, Morocco, is one case where local expertise cultivated through years of working on the historic preservation of the city took up the most challenging task of not only restoring a physical structure but integrating it into the social life of the city, while reasserting its role as a leading religious learning centre for both men and women. Another case at hand is the preservation of the city of Gjirokastra in Albania, where reclaiming the heritage of the city necessitated the assembly of scores of local and international experts. The work succeeded in forming a broad coalition of partners. The two projects highlight different approaches to understanding heritage as either a local tradition to be continued or a physical asset to be preserved. Each attitude had strengths and shortfalls. The debate on conservation should be enriched by such juxtapositions.

Another attempt at tackling the question of heritage comes from an unconventional project. The Souk Waqif in Qatar is a broad gesture for preserving local culture facing the rapidly globalising nature of modern cities. It is not a conservation project, because much of the original physical fabric was beyond preservation. But through thoughtful planning, the urban morphology was recreated and a major investment ensued to assure that this very rare sample of an urban heritage is preserved for future generations. A place was created to celebrate the diverse cultures that contributed to the creation of a modern state. An alternative to the generic shopping mall was opened to the residents of the city.

In contrast to the projects striving preserve a national asset, a tradition or the memory of a local culture, other projects challenged the whole notion of the indigenous. The Master Plan of the American University of Beirut and the Revitalisation of the Hypercentre of Tunis both aim to preserve heritage assets that reflect Western architectural traditions in cities with strong Muslim heritage. Yet both projects worked with the local populations and the end users preserve an essential part of the city. Choosing to recognise, celebrate and to preserve it marks not only a reconciliation with the colonial past but an acceptance of the city as a valid place to be. The whole world can learn from these two examples of how to carefully reweave the fabric of the city. At a time where instant history is being created by importing global brand-name developments on the fringes of sprawling conurbations, these two cases are shining examples of commitment to a genuine sense of place.

In an opposite direction, the museum of Madinat al-Zahra epitomises the need to view Muslim historiography as an integral part of the story of civilisation, and particularly Western civilisation. As shown by these last three examples, cultural history can be understood only by recognising its multicultural trajectories.

Treading lightly on earth is another theme that emerged from the shortlist. Projects posed very subtle questions to their contexts, whether it is the environment, the local culture or the city. They chose to open dialogue with their surroundings, and through a humble positioning of their built forms they contributed to challenging their local contexts. Rather than shouting, they whisper, which speaks eloquently to the modern world by exposing its limitations.

The Nishorgo Oirabot Nature Interpretation Centre in Bangladesh is a delicate insertion of a relatively large structure in the middle of the forest. It helps to communicate the need to preserve the natural environment to both locals and

Bridge School Xiashi Village, China

tourists. It borrows from a local building tradition the notion of raising itself on stilts, minimising its footprint. The Palmyra House on the western coast of India also provides a simple structure that blends with nature and demonstrates that luxury does not have to be intrusive. The same lesson can be learned at the Green School in Bali, Indonesia, where natural bamboo was used to develop a first-class learning institution, by simply raising major roof structures on armatures of bamboo.

The Dowlat II Residential Building in Tehran faces the street with a frontage of 6 metres, yet by refusing to succumb to the commercial pressure of middle-class housing, this humble porous facade supported by a simple framework challenges the whole city. In a similar gesture, the Chandgaon Mosque in Bangladesh opens up its geometry to accommodate the community through its sanctuary, challenging symbolic language by introducing innovative gestures based on a new reading of traditional forms: transparency as opposed to closure, scale rather than proportion and passage rather than destination.

While discussing the museum project at Madinat al-Zahra, the jury was reminded of an important cultural feature of Andalusia that is the context of the project. Historians often speak of a culture of *convivencia*, or living together, to describe the Muslim presence in Spain. Architecture can play a major role in bringing people to accept each other and to create spaces where living together is possible.

The Ipekyol Textile Factory in Edirne, Turkey, represents this important value of living together. Here people have to work closely together; they share the same space and breathe the same air. The architecture opens up the space and involves itself with the smallest details of the production line. Edirne is a city located at the crossroads between the Muslim and Western worlds, and the building defines a new age of economic complementarities between these two worlds. Its strength, however, stems from the fact that it can set standards of sensitive design for both. The building as a shared space is also exemplified by the Rubber Smokehouse in Malaysia. Through bringing together young people to work on recording the history of the small town of Lunas and its heritage, the building became a focus for ethnic reconciliation. Likewise, learning to explore the conditions of living together was exemplified in the Burkina Faso Women's Health Centre. The functions of the building are about coping with different perceptions of gender roles in a society, but the architecture also provides a symbolic umbrella that unifies the various rooms distinguished by different colours under the shade of the overarching roof. Forms and functions reinforce each other to create a space of empowerment for women.

The issues facing Muslim societies today are very diverse. The Award jury opted against recognising typologies or classes of building activities and favoured instead a deep exploration into why architecture and building activities take place. The celebrated projects have demonstrated a sensitive research into the ethical values that architecture faces today. But they were selected only when these sensitivities managed to produce an architecture of excellence in terms of design, meeting the needs of users, realising an impact beyond the site and involving the wider social and cultural milieu.

Some Reflections on Colonial Modernity / Postcolonial Realities and the Architecture of the Muslim World
Salah M. Hassan

Europe's colonies were never empty spaces to be made over in Europe's image or fashioned in its interests; nor indeed, were European states self-contained entities that at one point projected themselves overseas.
A.L. Stoler and F. Cooper, (1997)[1]

Since its commencement in 1977, the Aga Khan Award for Architecture has espoused originality and innovation in the diverse projects it sought to reward. As a jury member of its 2010 cycle, I had the fortune to witness first-hand the plurality of projects considered by the committee. A readiness to explore new frontiers of architecture of the Muslim world was apparent, and the inclusive vision of the Award serves as a powerful testament to the awareness of the multiplicity and diversity of Muslim societies. Undoubtedly this recognition was instrumental for grasping the nuances of spatiality and temporality, and their bearing on matters that surpass narrow national frontiers. The obvious attentiveness to both the complexity and dynamism of the Muslim world was the primary rationale undergirding the jury's deliberations. Several projects aiming at fulfilling the double tasks of preserving and revitalising architectural heritage—associated with the colonial period in several Muslim countries—have been considered in this current cycle. The inclusion of such wide-ranging projects is commendable, as it succeeded in foregrounding the central role of urban centres in former European colonies in North Africa, alongside other parts of the Islamic world, as sites of experimentation for Western modernist architects. It is common knowledge today that those early experimentations played a foundational role in the blossoming of these architects' careers.

As Mustafa Bayoumi reminds us, "The European colonial city was also a kind of 'virgin' space for European planners and architects, who took advantage of the opportunity to produce an entirely new built environment to test novel forms of urban planning linked to modern flows of colonial capital and goods, along with the allure of tourism and colonial migration".[2] Recent scholarship has demonstrated the critical role that colonial modernity has played in shaping the colonial city, and how colonial urban policy was topographically reproduced as a de facto apartheid system of segregated spaces in which the modern European sector stands as the "rational" model of planning in contrast to the "irrational" old Casbah (*qasbah* in Arabic), where the natives reside.[3] Works by scholars such as Gwendolyn Wright, in addition to recent interventions such as the exhibition "In the Desert of Modernity" and its companion book, *Colonial Modern*, illustrated how urban centres in colonial North Africa served since the 1930s as a laboratory for European modernists' utopianism and fantasies.[4]

A case in point was the city of Casablanca in Morocco. Casablanca was viewed as a test case for the "city of tomorrow" and a blueprint for European urban planning. The careers of modernist architects (such as Le Corbusier) and the housing projects on the outskirts of several European metropolises (such as Paris) could not have been possible without the colonial experimentation in North Africa.[6] French as well as British architecture and urban design in the colonies evolved over time as a series of adaptations that accompanied specific processes and patterns borne out of the metamorphosis of colonial policies. This phenomenon can be seen in the move from architectural styles imported directly from the European metropolis to newer ones that incorporated local architectural elements. The blueprint for such a move was written in earlier 19th-century Orientalists' visual and written texts that mimicked and documented local styles of the "Orient". Such semi-localised and hybrid architectural styles were later superseded by the introduction of a more modernist International Style during the last phase of colonial practices and power politics.

The common denominator in these fluctuating adaptive policies, as Gwendolyn Wright has explained—especially in the case of preserving local and traditional architectural elements in colonial urban design—was to maintain as well as buttress the superimposed colonial order of things. In some cases, the urge to include such local elements was a direct answer by colonial architects to resistance from locals to the new imposed forms and their longings for familiarity in a built environment they venerated.[6]

Resonances of this line of argument persist today as we ponder an Award recipient, the Revitalisation of the Hypercentre of Tunis. This project, as well as several shortlisted projects of the 2010 Award cycle, have been considered for their contributions to "promoting civil initiatives which are sensitive to issues of funding, the revitalisation of local economies, and their role in providing opportunities for local employment and training." As the jury citation reads, the significance of these projects also lies in the centrality of colonialism and its palpable role in shaping the urban built environment in North Africa, among other former colonies in the Muslim world. Some time has passed since the dawn of independence from colonial rule, and the significant transformations that followed have allowed spaces for critique and contemplative practices to assess, reflect and move forward.

As a jury member, I was struck by how colonial situations had helped engender a reconsideration of modernity and modernism. These categories have typically been constructed and studied without the critical discourse needed to evaluate their consequences for both theory and praxis. It is important at this juncture to invoke the work of Gwendolyn Wright again for its profound impact on the topic of colonialism. For instance, she reminds us that Western hegemony and the ideological force of imperialism have obscured the fact that "'Western' modernism came into being in a world framed by colonialism, where visions for improvement and innovation overlapped with and often caused brutal destruction. In the colonial world, as elsewhere, modernism was, and remains, at once a universal ambition, a transnational operation and myriad local variations".[7] Along with Wright, scholars such as Zeynep Çelik have ventured to offer useful insights into the intersections of colonialism and postcolonial memory. Çelik ably extended the French historian Pierre Nora's concept of *lieu de mémoire* —originally used in the context of French history—to the former French colonies in North Africa. The symbolic, functional and material significance of colonial sites, including architectural ones, was thoroughly explored. Mindful of how these sites act as "catalyst(s) in the imposition of a power structure, as well as the definition and endurance of identity in a colonial context", Çelik states that "the symbolic sites for the colonizer culture continued to maintain their significance in the postcolonial era as their capacity to change and acquire new meanings allowed them to act also as places of memory for the colonized".[8] The intersection of memory and history has been crucial in shaping how the colonised subject relates to past colonial sites and their evocation in the postcolonial present. As Çelik astutely pointed out, colonial sites have emerged as useful platforms for critiques of postcolonial realities.[9]

These realities prompt us to ask a series of questions about colonial modernity and postcolonial memory that are crucial as we probe the issue of modernity in light of pervasive postcolonial critiques. For example: How can one counter what seems to be the standard idea, which has privileged modernity as the West, but paradoxically also posited it as universal? What do we make of the inextricable link between colonialism and modernist utopias? What do we make of the colonial modernist projects given events and visions of decolonisation in North Africa and other parts of the Muslim world? And finally, what is the impact of such events in relation to the West itself, which has become more significantly multicultural than ever before in the context of recent Muslim diasporas in Europe and North America?

Postcolonial theory offers powerful critiques of modernity by showing how the terms of the debate are necessarily Eurocentric. Although modernity is better seen as irreducibly plural and fully global, standard theorisations of modernity and modernism, emphasising Western social transformations and artistic experiments, characterise social developments and artistic expressions of other regions as belated and secondary. In the same vein, Western hegemony has made us overlook that Western modernism and the unfolding of its history, from the Renaissance to the present, stands on the shoulders of other cultures and civilisations.[10] This glaring oversight has taken long to acknowledge, especially with regard to the artistic and literary contributions of decolonisation and opposition to imperialism.[11] On a positive note, recent scholarship on artistic and literary practices in the West has elucidated the increased epistemological uncertainty with which one must regard the contributions of non-Western and Muslim immigrant writers and artists to their host countries in the West. Rather than locating their production in a liminal space of "in between-ness", as has been the norm in European circles of art and literary criticism, new studies have called for a fresh understanding of contemporary European culture and cultural labor, and a serious rethinking of its spatial configuration.[12]

A most urgent issue is the current condition of the Muslim world in global politics. Post–September 11 developments have certainly heightened awareness of the interconnectedness and disjuncture between the "West" and the "Muslim" world. This is evident in the rise of Islamophobia and anti-immigration sentiments and legislation. Muslims, and more specifically those who are citizens of the West, found their loyalties to their countries being questioned.[14] We are suddenly faced with dichotomous thinking: "bad" Muslims, who practice terrorism and supposedly hate freedom and modernity (and oppress women), and "good" Muslims, who are modern, secular and support the policies of Western countries. As Mahmood Mamdani has argued, this premise is based on a culturalist approach to "Islam" that turns the latter into a transcendent category.[15] Accordingly, it is culture (modernity) that is said to be the dividing line between those in favour of a peaceful, civic existence and those inclined to terror. In this view, our world is split between those who are modern and those who are premodern.[13] Yet "Islam" is far from a homogeneous body of ritual and belief, and not all Muslims speak with the same voice. The dichotomy is both reductive and ahistorical: Not only does it absolve the West from having created the category of "bad" Muslims, but it also glosses over the multi-religious and multi-ethnic composition of the many regions in which Muslims live. Furthermore, it conceals a more complex history of indigenous modernist movements and anticolonial struggles augmented by indefatigable efforts by post-independence secular movements for democratisation, human rights, gender equality and sustainable development.[14]

The continued effort of the Aga Khan Award for Architecture becomes even more crucial in highlighting the existence of such diverse strands and promoting a grounded vision for peaceful and prosperous coexistence and fruitful intellectual exchange.

Notes
1. Ann Laura Stoler & Frederick Cooper, "Between Metropole and Colony: Rethinking a Research Agenda", in *Tensions of Empire: Colonial Encounters in a Bourgeois World*, edited by A.L. Stoler & F. Cooper. (Berekely & Los Angeles: University of California Press, 97), p. 1.
2. See Mustafa Bayoumi, "Shadows and Light: Colonial Modernity and the Grande Mosquée of Paris", *The Yale Journal of Criticism*, Vol.13, No. 2, Fall 2000, pp. 267–268.
3. Ibid.
4. See Gwendolyn Wright, *The Politics of Design in French Colonial Urbanism*, (University of Chicago Press, 1991); and *Colonial Modern: Aesthetics of the Past Rebellions for the Future*, edited by Tom Avermaete, Serhat Karakayali and Marion von Osten (London and Berlin: Black Dog Publishing and House of World Cultures, 2010).
5. See Wright, *Colonial Modern*.
6. See the introduction to Wright, *The Politics of Design in French Colonial Urbanism*, pp. 1–13.
7. Gwendolyn Wright, "Building Global Modernisms", *Grey Room*, No. 7 (Spring 2002), p.125.
8. Zeynep Celik, "Colonial/Postcolonial Intersections: Lieux de Memoire in Algeria", *Third Text Asia*, Issue 2, Spring 2009, pp. 43–56.
9. See Edward Said, *Culture and Imperialism* (New York: Alfred Knopf, 1993), p. 242; and Salah M. Hassan, "African Modernism: Beyond Alternative Modernities Discourse", *SAQ: South Atlantic Quarterly*, 109:3 (Summer 2010), pp. 451–476.
10. Edward Said, *Culture and Imperialism*, p. 242.
11. Leslie Adelson, "Manifesto of 'Against Betweenness'", in *Unpacking Europe: A Critical Reader*, edited by Salah M. Hassan and Iftikhar Dadi (Rotterdam: NAi and Museum Boijmans Van Beuningen, 2001), p. 244–255.
12. Salah M. Hassan, "Contemporary 'Islamic' Art and Western Curatorial Politics of Representation in Post 9/11", *The Future of Tradition/Traditions of the Future*, edited by Chris Dercon, Leon Krempel and Avinaom Shalem. (Munich: Prestel and Haus de Kunst, 2010), pp. 35–42.
13. See Samuel Huntington's *Clash of Civilizations and the Remaking of the World Order* (New York: Simon Schuster, 1998); Bernard Lewis, *What Went Wrong with Islam* (Oxford: Oxford University Press and Harper Perennial Books, 2003); and Bernard Lewis, "The Root of Muslim Rage", *Atlantic Monthly*, September (1990).
14. Somewhat paradoxically perhaps, the period since 9/11 has also witnessed a renewed interest in modern art movements and contemporary artists of both Muslim and Arab backgrounds and of Middle Eastern and North African origins.

Revitalisation of the Hypercentre of Tunis, Tunisia

On Advocacy
Omar Abdulaziz Hallaj

Over the last thirty years, the Aga Khan Award for Architecture has recognised excellence in interventions in the built environment. The Award has brought to light examples and best practices of projects that then served as inspiration for architects, designers, planners, engineers, decision makers, community organisers and most important, communities everywhere in the Muslim world. At the end of each cycle, the juries delivered not just a decision on winning projects but a benchmark for new trends and important issues facing Muslim communities. Inadvertently, the Award did more than recognize models of architecture; it contributed to a discourse on the way that societies are defined, their processes elaborated and their economic and social capitals evolved.

The Award has sought to use the winning projects as a platform for debate and for engagement of professionals and decision makers everywhere. The winning projects, cast as role models, were instrumental in generating technical know-how, insights for architectural education and deeper appreciation of community resources and needs. Despite the fact that each jury issued eloquent statements to explain its choices, the diversity of projects chosen inadvertently overwhelmed the reasons for their selection. At the heart of each cycle was the meticulous elaboration of a citation for the winning projects that identified innovative aspects; indirectly, the citations highlighted how each project can be viewed as a role model for others. The Award was communicating the value of individual projects, yet the overall value of the winning projects was conveyed as secondary. Nonetheless, that value accumulated cycle after cycle and evolved into a basic image of the Award as a promoter of local community identities and creative responses to limited resources, as well as excellence in design.

The juries' ethical stances in selecting the winning projects were often implied and not elucidated directly. Occasionally, the juries tried to interject their interpretations of the ethics behind each winning project, but were not very transparent about the ethics of the selection process itself. The Award does not endorse particular ethical positions but aims to promote diversity. This proved to be one of the most prominent features of the Award as an open, inclusive system. Yet by refraining from foregrounding ethical concerns, the Award has not helped to promote an open debate on ethics in the built environment.

Winning projects were mostly discussed as inspirations and best practices. There was no focus on these projects becoming replicable or scalable, and for good reason. What distinguished these projects was the fact that they refused to accept standard solutions and developed special responses to their particular challenges. But there must be an intrinsic value in the winning projects serving as models, or otherwise there is little value in the Award. This is where the discussion on ethics must be brought to bear, not by adopting particular ethical positions but by expanding the ethical debates around architecture.

The ethical decisions of the jury must be placed in the open and debated at large. It is not sufficient to recognize a project that supports the reinvigoration of public space in the city. The whole value of public space must be debated. What does the category "public" mean? This was one example of our debate as a jury for this cycle. If we put private space to public use without having the public rights and freedoms, can we still be speaking of public space? The issue gets complicated if privatisation is the only way to secure funding for preserving public space. What are the guarantees of the public domain? Why have public institutions failed to develop the mechanisms for preserving public space?

Other questions could be: Why do we preserve the environment? What is the nature of our responsibility and custodianship over the environment? This cycle, the jury summarised that argument under the rubric of "treading lightly on earth", borrowing a metaphor from the Quran regarding how the faithful must be humble and accepting of the transience of the world. How do we transform these values into ethical questions in our building practices? The Award is certainly not responsible to provide answers but it should play a more proactive role in presenting these questions for discussion. This is what I would like to designate as an advocacy role for the Award, a role not yet fully developed. The Award is neither an implementer of projects nor an educational or academic institution. It has a capacity to advocate for a deeper and more complex debate on the ethics of the built environment. Its main strength is that it has built over the years a very strong communications platform, a platform that speaks to laypeople, practitioners, academics and decision makers alike. Although this platform is important, it is not focused. One of the key aspects of communications strategy is to define focused messages for particular constituencies and around special issues. An advocacy role will require the Award to use its communications tools to focus on ethical debates and to leverage the impact of these debates.

Of course, communication is a two-way street. The leveraging of communications should not be just to disseminate the outcome of debates but to expand the inclusiveness of the debate and open up participation. The Steering Committee has so far provided the Award with global direction. Much of its esteemed role has been informed by the contributions of its experienced members—some bring fresh ideas, while others provide institutional memory. How much of the strategic direction of the Award's steering is informed by the community, academic and media activities developed in between Award cycles? Of course a great deal of influence is possible through the participation of Steering Committee and jury members in these activities. But how systemic is that influence? This is another area where an advocacy role for the Award would work on entrenching the outcomes of the communications platforms into the strategic direction of the Award.

The Award has typically emphasized the winning project as a model of excellence. Perhaps in the future, the Award should also be interested in recognising the excellence in solutions that feature innovation in replication, scalability, economies of scale and a realistic understanding of the magnitude of challenges that Muslim societies face. An advocacy role for the Award should move beyond the aesthetics of the winning project to the ethics of handling major challenges. One idea is to enhance the jury with more expertise from fields such as economics and social services. A well-balanced jury would engage debates on issues such as feasibility, impact, opportunity costs, cost-benefit analysis and human resource development in addition to aesthetics, response to site, technical know-how, environmental sensibility and cultural relevance.

Thirty years ago, when the world was paying the price of the International Style's homogenising effects on local cultures, the Award set for itself the challenging task of identifying excellent local interventions that resisted hegemonic global trends. Today the world is threatened by relativist attitudes towards the local. The Award must respond by making local solutions relevant as answers to global challenges. An advocacy position would entail a shift from focusing on the winning project as a model to the winning project as a gateway for ethical solutions.

On-Site Review: Excursions into Ethnographic Architectural Criticism
Gökhan Karakuş

In 1958 the French anthropologist and sociologist Pierre Bourdieu published an account of his fieldwork in Algeria in his first book, *Sociologie de l'Algérie*.[1] This important study of the traditional social structures of Algeria included one of the first ethnographic analyses of architecture and domesticity in post–World War II society. Six years later, the Museum of Modern Art in New York presented an exhibition entitled "Architecture Without Architects: A Short Introduction to Non-Pedigreed Architecture", organised by the critic Bernard Rudofsky, that provided a demonstration of the artistic, functional and cultural richness of various types of autochthonous architecture such as vernacular, anonymous and archetypal. Local and vernacular architecture was proposed as a kind of contemporary architecture, a viable alternative to the modernist architecture of the day.

Between Bourdieu's initial intellectual forays into the contemporary social role of autochthonous architecture and "Architecture Without Architects"' wide-ranging survey, there occurred a major transformation of the role of architecture in society. Architecture—having gone through a radical reappraisal at the beginning of the 20th century, rejecting tradition in favour of industry and the machine aesthetic—was starting to come to terms with the reality of how this "revolution" might apply not only to the West but to the whole world. Modern architecture as a catalyst in the transformation to a global system was confronted with a diversity of cultures and environments that challenged many of its basic principles.

This transformation was one of the first signs of a unifying global postwar culture, economy and politics. The Cold War, consumerism, high-speed transportation and the electronic revolution in media and telecommunications all contributed to the formation of a new global consciousness. No longer limited by geography, millions of people could see how those in other parts of the world lived. The communications theorist Marshall McLuhan, in his book *The Gutenberg Galaxy* from 1962, described this emerging world in terms of a "global village". In the early 1960s, McLuhan wrote that visual, individualistic print culture would soon be brought to an end by what he described as "electronic interdependence". In this new era, he proclaimed, humankind would move from individualism and fragmentation to a collective identity, with a "tribal base". McLuhan described this global village in both negative and positive terms, using technological and anthropological metaphors:

Instead of tending towards a vast Alexandrian library the world has become a computer, an electronic brain, exactly as an infantile piece of science fiction. And as our senses have gone outside us, Big Brother goes inside. So, unless aware of this dynamic, we shall at once move into a phase of panic terrors, exactly befitting a small world of tribal drums, total interdependence, and superimposed co-existence. [...] In our long striving to recover for the Western world a unity of sensibility and of thought and feeling we have no more been prepared to accept the tribal consequences of such unity than we were ready for the fragmentation of the human psyche by print culture.[2]

The global village concept drew comparisons between an emerging universal, utopian modern architecture and the variety of ways of living in traditional settings in autochthonous and vernacular architectures. While formalised modern architecture provided a vision for contemporary living, the anthropological thinking characteristic of Bourdieu's method and the MoMA exhibition by Rudofsky exposed the contemporary realities of living for a greater number of peoples and places.

In the preface to the "Architecture Without Architects" catalogue, Rudofsky contrasted "the serenity of the architecture in so-called underdeveloped countries with the architectural blight in industrial countries".[3] In the emerging global village, "Architecture Without Architects" was a step towards a critical and ideological justification of living in the contemporary and the traditional at the same time. In this important moment in the development of modern architecture, this exhibition included the profound call to conceive of these autochthonous architectures—vernacular, anonymous, archetypal—within a wider conception of modern architecture.

The critical and popular view proposed by this anthropological critique of modern life would quickly in the mid-1960s turn into a more radical challenge to the dominant practice of modern architecture. Robert Venturi's *Complexity and Contradiction in Architecture*[4] (a MoMA publication) appeared in 1966 as a foundational document that would usher in the age of the postmodern. Like Rudofsky, Venturi showed that alternatives existed in the contemporary uses of local, autochthonous architectures, especially the vernacular. In the spirit of the socially minded 1960s, vernacular architecture emerged as a counterpoint to modern architecture in a debate about the effects of the latter on how people were living.

We cannot underestimate the more general questioning of conventional notions of architecture and dwelling through autochthonous, local and vernacular building techniques and alternative ways of living posed in the late 1950s and early 1960s. This theme has resurfaced in architectural theory since then, in many contexts. Among related ideas were Christopher Alexander's concept of "pattern language" of the late 1970s, and Alexander Tzonis and Liane Lefaivre's "Critical Regionalism" from 1981,[5] further advanced by Kenneth Frampton in his essay "Towards a Critical Regionalism: Six Points for an Architecture of Resistance"[6] in 1983 and in the reactionary "New Urbanism" movement of the 1980s. The analysis of Lagos, Nigeria, by Rem Koolhaas that appeared in his book *Mutations* in 2001 shared this fascination with the urbanised vernacular of squatter settlements.[7] Another MoMA exhibition, "Small Scale, Big Change: New Architectures of Social Engagement" of late 2010, looks at "radically pragmatic" locally minded, socially oriented architecture, primarily in Latin America, Africa and Asia.

But perhaps one of the most important exegeses of the vernacular in contemporary life was a work outside of the Western context: Hassan Fathy's utopian vision for rural architecture in Gourna, Egypt, published in 1969 and later in English as *Architecture for the Poor: An Experiment in Rural Egypt*.[8] Fathy's ideas on the vernacular, infused with a detailed ethnographic understanding, became a point of reference that we can identify in today's thinking on sustainable architecture. His architecture might not have had the widespread influence in his time that he had hoped for, but it did generate consideration of new approaches to what kind of architecture people should live in, not just in the urbanised, industrialised West but in rural and agrarian parts of the world. Fathy's ideas allowed for the emergence of a system to value these nonformal architectures as responses to the needs of contemporary habitation. In this way, his intellectual weight was also instrumental in the emergence of the Aga Khan Award for Architecture, with Fathy being honoured with its Chairman's Award in the First Cycle of the Award in 1980.

With the Award, there has been a pragmatic broadening of the argument on socially minded architecture. Throughout its history, the Award has been deeply concerned with how people live in the many contexts of the Islamic world, whether urban, rural, institutional or traditional. The Award has provided meaningful architectural examples to villages and agrarian areas, and equally to airports, offices, factories, technical projects and landscapes in its wide assessment of the built environment. Today the Award vision of sustainability and advanced design is providing a way forward to solve some of the pressing issues that face not only the larger populations of Asia and Africa that are starting to undergo their version of modernisation but the Western, industrialised world as well.

Bangladesh 2010, Aga Khan Award for Architecture On-Site Review
The ethnographic experience of contemporary architecture presents a compelling conflation of old and new. Contemporary architecture, not yet worn by use, contains the hope for a new space of life and habitation. This potential of contemporary architecture gives it a utopian character, as a world visible but not yet completely formed. Contemporary architecture in traditional societies poses the challenge of how to coordinate this contemporaneity with the reality of established customs. Particularly in rural and agrarian contexts, this becomes a negotiation between the established practices of the local culture

and the forces of the contemporary. In this relationship emerges the larger question of modernity as a meaningful social practice in the lives of people around the world—how this modernity interacts with what were previously seen as small, circumscribed, isolated and "authentic" traditional societies.

The Aga Khan Award for Architecture's review process presents a unique opportunity to understand how everyday life is synthesised around the ideas of place and modernity in the 21st century. Here we are speaking of a move past the reductivist thinking that views people who inhabit traditional places as not part of the modern world. This is an important aspect of the Aga Khan Award for Architecture's larger task of promoting raised living standards in urban and rural settings, in places of both tradition and modernity in the contemporary Islamic world. As outlined in the Award charter, it is a process that emphasises architecture that provides for people's physical, social and economic needs, and also responds to their cultural and spiritual expectations.

The Award gives particular attention to building schemes that use local resources and appropriate technology in an innovative way, and to projects likely to inspire similar efforts elsewhere. This is all done to meet the goal of modernisation, but within a sensitive and sustainable understanding of how people can live. Within these parameters, the Award can just as meaningfully be given to an airport terminal design based on advanced tensile architecture, the urban renewal of a city's fabric that dates from many eras, and handmade constructions by local villagers.

To recognise these dynamics of the modern and the local as a method of architectural criticism requires a type of anthropological thinking called proximate ethnography,[9] an understanding of how contemporary life can be formed between the modern and the traditional, advancing past defunct concepts such as the exotic and the underdeveloped. The task of proximate ethnography or an ethnography of the modern world is to see the analyst as part of the culture under analysis, in a performative way. Modernity and tradition are treated the same. Architectural criticism utilising this ethnographic perspective puts the act of criticism in the same ethnological frame as the buildings and societies under analysis.

The advantage here is that the exercise is not one of an advanced global agent leading the locals but a collective act of analysis and architectural discourse. The task is both to understand the building and society under review and to think about how one's activities as an analyst are an integral part of the process of conceiving of modern architecture. As a reviewer, one is part of a global network of architects, writers and teachers responsible for the cooperative advancement of 21st-century discourse. Stepping into the field as part of the On-Site Review, the responsibility to both represent the discourse of the Award and be one of the ones forming it becomes extremely clear.

The process of the On-Site Review is one of encounter and constant negotiation with a local culture that is part of the architectural critique of the project under review. In other words, the review has the potential to provide a crucial intermediary step in the progression of ideas from hypotheses to theories to built form. At its most basic, the review requires an assessment in situ of a building in a foreign culture. At increasing levels of complexity, the review becomes a highly charged encounter with insular societies and their difficult internal dynamics and relations, with architecture as the subject and the reviewer as a quasi authority.

For me personally, the foreign context was made legible by my history and familiarity with Islamic and traditional agrarian societies. In this way, it was partly for me an excursion into a proximate ethnography. I was involved in the everyday society of Bangladesh as an analyst and architectural critic. But at the same time, I operated as though I were a local, to better understand the uses that this architecture was having in a simple, everyday way.

This constant modulation in role and activity, especially feeling connected to the local, is an important part of the Award. Being "in the field", inside the societies that use the contemporary architecture, gives the Award a perspective that goes beyond the evaluation system of other architectural awards. Instead of plans and perspectives reviewed by a jury far away from the building, you have an On-Site Reviewer interacting with the local society in many ways, in many contexts. An opportunity for ethnographic architectural criticism and discourse arises constantly. The reviewer disseminates ideas to a variety of people at different points in the social strata, in diverse positions of power and influence, affecting thinking on the subject.

One important aspect of this interaction is the relationship of the On-Site Reviewer with the architects of the project. For me these were Ehsan Khan of Vitti Sthapati Brindo Ltd., architects of the Nishorgo Oirabot Nature Interpretation Centre, and Kashef Chowdury, architect of Chandgaon Mosque—two shortlisted projects of the 2010 Award Cycle. These regional architects with global perspectives understood my predisposition to see the review as both an ethnographic and an architectural analysis. They guided me in the local culture, but were careful to allow me to experience the buildings first-hand. I was able to judge their projects architecturally, but also to see how these architects and their buildings performed technically and socially. Sometimes their interaction with the builders, clients and users became more important than the building itself. In some cases, the cooperation provided by the On-Site Review team (the architect, a local photographer/architect and a translator/architect) allowed the opportunity to move away from Western-based rational analyses altogether. Given such detailed understanding of the workings of the local society, the close relations between the Bangladeshi villagers and the team (all of Bangladeshi origin except for me) permitted us to jump into a symbolic and spiritual register, to a more narrative exploration of place, nature and habitation.

Notes

1 Pierre Bourdieu, *Sociologie de l'Algérie* (Paris: Presses Universitaires de France, 1958).
2 Marshall McLuhan, *The Gutenberg Galaxy: The Making of Typographic Man* (Toronto: University of Toronto Press, 1962), p. 32.
3 Bernard Rudofsky, *Architecture Without Architects: A Short Introduction to Non-Pedigreed Architecture* (New York: Museum of Modern Art, 1964), p. 3.
4 Robert Venturi, *Complexity and Contradiction in Architecture,* with an introduction by Vincent Scully (New York: Museum of Modern Art, 1966).
5 "The Grid and the Pathway: The Work of D. and S. Antonakakis", *Architecture in Greece 15,* 1981.
6 Kenneth Frampton, "Towards a Critical Regionalism: Six Points for an Architecture of Resistance", in *The Anti-Aesthetic: Essays on Postmodern Culture,* edited by Hal Foster (Port Townsend, WA: Bay Press, 1983).
7 Rem Koolhaas, Stefano Boeri, Sanford Kwinter, Nadia Tazi, Hans Ulrich Obrist, et al., *Mutations* (Barcelona: Actar, 2001).
8 Hassan Fathy, *Architecture for the Poor: An Experiment in Rural Egypt* (Chicago: University of Chicago Press, 1976).
9 Michael Sherringham, *Everyday Life: Theories and Practices from Surrealism to the Present* (New York: Oxford University Press, 2006), p. 293.

Madinat al-Zahra Museum Cordoba, Spain

Landscape as Ecological Infrastructure for an Alternative Urbanity
Yu Kongjian

I am glad that the jury has selected the Wadi Hanifa Wetlands for the Aga Khan Award because this project embodies a powerful practice: the recovery of landscape as ecological infrastructure, as an alternative way to build our cities.

Civilisation, over the course of centuries, has been defined in part as the control of natural processes and patterns: those who were successful in exploiting natural resources and transforming natural patterns through technological advancements were considered highly civilised, while those who adapted to natural forces were seen as primitive. Cities are by far the largest and most complicated artificial devices that human beings have constructed, and they are considered by many to be the very testament of human civilisation. From the origin of the city to its "modernised" form today, natural forces and patterns have become increasingly controlled and dependent on artificial processes. The quality of urbanity becomes measured by how quickly rain-water drains off our streets, how stable temperature and humidity are maintained in our rooms (or even in open spaces), how garden trees and shrubs are grown for ornamental purposes rather than for their productivity.

Over time, we have drifted away from nature and become disconnected from our roots as farmers and herders. This standard of civilisation is built on heavily engineered gray infrastructure: complicated transportation systems designed for vehicles to deliver goods and services; huge pipe networks laid underground to drain excess storm water; rivers reinforced with concrete walls to control floods; large sewage plants built to treat wastewater; power lines to convey the energy necessary to run all of the machines and devices. Built upon this gray infrastructure are showy buildings with deformed heads and twisted bodies that deviate from what natural forces would allow.

Such a model of urbanity, created by Western cities during the early stages of their development, has unfortunately been adopted today by developing countries in general and the Islamic world in particular. Here, landscape is largely limited to tamed gardens and parks, where lawns and flowers are irrigated with tap water and storm water is drained by underground pipes. Here, landscape is just like other components of an artificial city—a sink of energy and services, rather than a source. Landscape as a natural ecosystem in and around cities is largely neglected, its natural processes disintegrated and contaminated, and its natural patterns fragmented. The landscape completely loses its capacity to provide what would have been free goods and services for urban communties.

What would an alternative city look like if its natural forces were respectfully used and not controlled? Vegetables and food would be produced along streets or in parks, floods would come and go to the benefit of the city, waste would be absorbed and cleansed by natural processes, birds and other native species would cohabit the city with human beings, and the beauty of nature would be appreciated in its authenticity, not tamed or tightly maintained. This alternative practice has many names: agricultural urbanism, landscape urbanism, water urbanism, new urbanism, sustainable urbanism, green urbanism, and certainly ecological urbanism. The key here is that these alternative solutions do not rely on gray infrastructure but instead utilise green or ecological infrastructure to deliver the goods and services that the city and its urban residents need.

Looking at the history of city planning and building, we find that traditional designs treat landscape as one physical and organisational entity, rather than as isolated ornamental pieces. Most cultures, and Islamic culture in particular, have a pre-scientific tradition of using geomancy to organise settlements based on the idea that a sacred landscape includes both spiritual and physical infrastructure. Since the late 19th century, the United States has used parks and green spaces as fundamental infrastructures to address urban problems such as congestion and sanitation. More recently, this concept of greenways was further developed into a more comprehensive and interconnected framework called green infrastructure, which is considered the basis for "urban form" within urbanising and metropolitan regions. In early 20th-century Europe, greenbelt, green heart and green wedge were used by urban designers in growing cities as stoppers, separators and connecters of urban development and to create a good urban form. Today, similar ecological networks are planned for metropolitan areas across Europe.

It is extremely important to caution urban decision makers in the developing world about mistakes made in the past by Western development. It is essential to understand that although the developed Western cities are now cleaning up by restoring green urbanism traditions, they are having to address the damage done to the urban environment during the 20th century. Their current adaptive solutions are mindful of global climate change and environmental sustainability. If we disregard the lessons learned, then the later developing and urbanising world will simply repeat the same mistakes that Western countries made, but at a much larger scale. Our decision makers need to understand that being later urbanised and developed provides opportunities to build better cities that enable better lives; but this is only possible if the alternative urbanism approach is chosen over the 20th-century North American urbanism model. The key here is that the planning and design of ecological infrastructure needs to happen before urban development, or as soon as possible.

Ecological infrastructure can be understood as the necessary structure of a sustainable landscape (or ecosystem) in which the output of goods and services is maintained and the capacity of systems to deliver those same goods and services to future generations is not undermined. What makes the concept of ecological infrastructure a powerful tool for advancing ecological urbanism is its marriage with the understanding of ecosystem services. Four categories of services are commonly identified: provisioning, related to the production of food and clean water; regulating, related to the control of climate and disease, and the mediation of flood and drought; supporting, related to nutrient cycles and providing habitat for wild plant and animal species; and cultural, related to spiritual and recreational benefits.

It is important to recognise that the conventional approach to urban development planning, based on population projections, built infrastructure and architectural objects, is unable to meet the challenges and needs of an ecological and sustainable urban form. Conventionally, landscape and green elements are usually negatively defined by architectural and built infrastructure. By positively defining ecological infrastructure for the sake of ecosystem services and the cultural integrity of the land, the urban growth pattern and urban form are negatively defined. Ecological infrastructure builds a bridge between ecological urbanism, the disciplines of ecology (and especially landscape ecology), the notion of ecosystem services and sustainable development. It is the bridge between smart development and smart conservation.

The Wadi Hanifa Wetlands project stands as an example, albeit not a perfect one, of how a neglected landscape can be recovered as an ecological infrastructure. It offers an alternative method to gray infrastructure in restoring and enhancing natural systems' capacity to provide multiple ecosystem services, including cleaning contaminated water, mediating flood and drought, providing habitats for native biodiversity, as well as creating spiritual and recreational benefits. It is a step in the right direction for an alternative ecological urbanism.

Wadi Hanifa Wetlands Riyadh, Saudi Arabia

Reuniting Processes and Product: Lessons for the Built Environment
Hanif Kara

A Story within a Story
Good design needs to be recognised with awards of this stature to ensure that merit triumphs over mediocrity, good over bad, and to prove that investment in quality buildings and infrastructure can generate further societal wealth. The recipients of such rewards can often act as agents of change, encouraging others to emulate their achievements with the same conviction, creativity and intelligence, risking resources without certainty of outcome, to build better places for the common good. Furthermore, this Award's process, by its nature, has the ability to prove that the story behind a project is often as important as the project itself—and this Award cycle reiterates that point as strongly as any preceding it.

The Award's ability to get to the core values of a project has a lot to do with the nature of the judging process—the three-year cycle of scrutiny to which all nominees must submit. The experience is increasingly rewarding over time, for those involved in the process, as a scheme becomes exposed to ever-greater levels of magnification. Judging begins with initial assessments of schemes, based purely on images and "sound bites" from the architect or client, but as these pass under the eyes of the Steering Committee, Master Jury, the Aga Khan Award team and review panels, information is filtered and clearer views begin to form. But it is the rigorous On-Site Review process that differentiates the AKAA from other more superficial awards, as it leads one beyond mere image or curiosity to the very root of the project. And it is from this root that the true stories of the winning buildings emerge—although each can have more than one story.

This iterative process of compounding and assimilating information over time seems analogous with evolutionary biologist Richard Dawkins's coining of the term "meme" in his 1976 book, *The Selfish Gene*,[1] a word articulating the concept of a self-replicating cultural idea that modifies human behaviour, perceptions or attitudes—small shifts that collectively can induce seismic societal changes. But why is this concept applicable to this Award? Previously the Award has most often been given to publicly funded projects for the developing world, used mainly by the public, but with the Ipekyol Textile Factory clothing factory in Edirne, Turkey, one may hypothesise that the same criteria might be just as applicable to the private sector.

In previous judging cycles, the Award has never been conferred on a factory building; but then again, this is no ordinary factory. Furthermore, it has taken many Award cycles (over 30 years) to slowly shift attitudes in the regions amongst clients and architects, and within juries that encourage this relatively "new type" of building to be nominated and considered. Factories affect societies and can rightly be included for an award that premiates good design, alongside the more commonly featured building types such as museums, cultural buildings, schools and houses.

In the less developed world, clothing production, predominantly for the Western market, is associated with sweatshops—large, anonymous factories located in sheds on the urban periphery, with appalling working conditions, at the blunt end of a fragmented production process. Within their walls, there is little or no enduring technology transfer, and with the product's true value being realised only in the country of consumption, no real contribution in taxes to the economies of the host nation. Meanwhile, the nature of the production line means that not only are modern consumption demands met through facilities that alienate workers from each other and from the products they produce, but the fragmentary production process ensures that a holistic quality-control process is next to nonexistent.

Ipekyol, on the other hand, is an aspirational brand, and its chairman, Yalçin Ayaydin, is nothing if not a visionary. His own childhood in a family of garment workers gave him an intimate knowledge of the business, one that he would later use to build his own fabric company and eventual clothing empire. Ipekyol started manufacturing clothes for the great fashion houses of Europe, where there is a heavy emphasis on product quality, but recently the firm realised that its brand need not work under these companies, but could compete on a par, creating more wealth-generation potential for the owner and the country. One might read the construction of this factory then as nothing but a sound commercial decision from an owner who, after collecting feedback from consumers, decided that if the highest quality was to be maintained, the whole production process would have to be brought under one roof. Yet this "one-stop" factory resists the temptation to favour the commodity/consumer relationship and instead reinforces that of the producer/commodity. From this one decision, possibly in memory of the owner's childhood, has transpired a microeconomic social agenda for the brand resulting in a retail product and physical workplace that both thrive on design.

Situationism and the "Factory Girl"

Machines, like prickles /
Sink into her heart every day
Her hands that should knit wools /
are breadwinning every day
Every evening at sunset /
A girl passes my door
Turns the corner and disappears /
with her head bowed tiredly
She rolls tobacco in the factory /
as if she smokes herself
Dreaming while rolling /
Like all human beings do...
—From "Factory Girl"
by Turkish singer Alplay

Of course, such a social vision needs a visionary to give it form. At one point, I asked about the main inspirations of the factory's architect, Emre Arolat—a question that practitioners like to pose to gain insight into others' thinking, and to dispel any personal preconceptions about the work. Without being explicit, he told me of Guy Debord's infamous Situationist text, *The Society of the Spectacle*,[2] which I quickly revisited to find this quote: "Commodities are all there is to see—the world we see is a world of commodity." Similarly, journalist Nina Rappaport refers to contemporary centres of production, where, for example, in the luxury automobile industry, the consumer is allowed to watch part of the production process as a "pre-consumption experience", in "spectacular factories".[3] By contrast, the outsourcing manufacturers, such as the workshops and warehouses for Nike and GAP or indeed most of the factories in Turkey, would be considered "anti-spectacular" factories. Neither classification, however, fits the unique character of the Ipekyol Textile Factory, as neither prioritises the worker over the consumer—whether in terms of "exclusivity" or "best value".

In my view, Debord's cry for some form of cultural revolution is echoed in Arolat's design. At Ipekyol Textile Factory, Modernist "Bauhaus" references are palpable, but sound reasoning can be posited for the choice of this architectural style. The formal look is delivering a rare message for the typology—here the form follows the function of the worker. There is a frugal but intrinsic quality to the choice of materials, enhancing the working experience of the users, the image and brand of the product, while presenting a strong public face to the eventual consumers.

The Consequential Effect—
Making the Building
As a holistic synergy between client and architect, this qualitative shift in the conventional factory typology is achieved through a number of approaches, with a level of poetry evident in all of them. Completing this part of the bigger story is the fact that despite the choice of the Modern idiom, all materials used in the making of the building were procured within Turkey. Local industry and employment were supported through the decision not to outsource the modern cladding system, or indeed any materials. The design also exhibits no reliance on trendy (and more expensive) systems and is carried out without resorting to less modern approaches taken by comparable facilities in Turkey. Arolat realised economies in dealing with seismic loads by adopting an even distribution of columns without bold, ambitious spans—a smart, pragmatic response for dealing with the issue, one that is worryingly often either ignored altogether or handled with the kind of overengineering only justified by the software power of finite element analysis.

But it is in the formal layout that this building's social awareness is most evident. Counterpointing the appropriate industrial aesthetic of the general cladding, the generous, cool and light-glazed entrance foyer connects the building with its context and acts as its shop front. Beyond this are the training rooms where recruits can take three-month courses that give them the skills base to increase their chances of working within the industry—a pedagogic tool to promote the industry in an area long associated with fabric production. Beyond this, changing, toilet and canteen facilities are spacious, well designed and scrupulously clean. Light wells in the administrative areas double as natural ventilation shafts, as well as acting as breakout spaces for workers. And on the factory floor, the architect's choice of a high and deep form exponentially transforms the space, creating a bright and airy, naturally ventilated space that has both grace and dignity.

Throughout, visual communication is inherent in the spatial strategy and design aesthetic in a manner intended to break down the social hierarchy between blue- and white-collar workers, and in an industry usually characterised by a predominantly female workforce and male managers, between male and female; the "Factory Girl" is no longer pigeonholed. This "one-stop" factory is a multivalent, inclusive design that incorporates forms and approaches that embody a deeper understanding of not only the needs of the local economy and the commercial factors that drive the clothing industry (digital technologies, economies of space and speed of production) but the social aspects too. The project is also a call for "inclusive design" in the East for facilities that are used mainly by female workers, although putting the words "inclusive" and "design" together has the potential for seeming like a contradiction; popular design thinking tends to promote individual creation and often celebrates those who develop unique visual language in a process that runs counter to the idea of inclusiveness. Ultimately, in a way that still generates profit for the owner, the Ipekyol facility is about nothing less than transforming the "Factory Girl's" life.

Many Birds, One Stone
This story concludes with getting "many birds with one stone". Through mediation and appropriation of a client's vision, materiality, branding, geography, localism, inclusivity, technology and architecture, progress and social wealth are restored to the garment factory worker while value accrues to the business owner. It was like that once, before the domination of consumer society, when the physical process of design and making was linked to a common sense of purpose and benefit. Today, for instance, "manufacturing as a nation" in developed countries is unlikely to be restored—it is gone, and perhaps forever. From this, developing countries could learn that the division of process and products was a last lament and try to hold onto the honesty of "making". In the built environment, occasionally the AKAA is mistakenly thought to award only old building types—in refurbishments or restorations. Restoring the "old" or making the "new" must not be viewed as the automatic path to progress on its own. Why should the developing world "make do" with what it has at hand (old buildings that need conserving)? Yet equally, the developing world should not resort to "flattening" history and territorialising the lands with new buildings. The Ipekyol Textile Factory could be seen as an exemplar—a possibility for a different future for factories in the region. Often changes created by new mass genres (modern construction, in this case) are widely considered an assault on civilisation or culture and labeled "marginal noise", to be dismissed. A case in point is the "boom-box mixers" of New York's Bronx, which were once similarly dismissed but today are recognised as the forefathers of "hip hop". Much earlier, the songs of the Beatles were dismissed because of their "newness" and reliance on new technologies. This factory too could be dismissed as "marginal noise".

The Ipekyol Textile Factory came from a private conviction funded by a commercial venture and was designed predominantly for the use of factory workers. On a global scale, such an approach is rare, demanding courage and commitment from the client and the architect to fight the relentless march of pure production logic in factories today, which proceeds without an understanding of its ultimate consequences. With a little imagination, perhaps the Ipekyol Textile Factory suggests an alternative ending to this otherwise sadly familiar tale.

Notes
1. Richard Dawkins, *The Selfish Gene* (Oxford: Oxford University Press, 1976).
2. Guy Debord, *The Society of the Spectacle*, translated by Fredy Perlman (Detroit: Black and Red, 1977).
3. Nina Rappaport, "The Consumption of Production", *Praxis*, issue 5, Architecture after Capitalism, 2003.

Ipekyol Textile Factory Edirne, Turkey

What About Symbols?
Farshid Moussavi

Architecture, given its public nature, is intrinsically cultural. In our globalised world, however, the nature of culture is changing so rapidly that the traditional meaning of this term is no longer valid. Culture used to represent a set of values and conventions developed among a particular group of people and validated by consensus. Today culture is no longer attached to a specific place or time. As it constantly adapts to shifting values, mores and ethics, culture has become a kind of theatre of movement in which the processes of change in everyday life are expressed in a variety of forms, and it is these forms which unite, or coalesce, their diverse audiences by providing them with shared experiences.

Beginning with the Golden Age of the 8th century, when many isolated regions and civilisations began to be integrated into Islamic civilisation, Muslims were among the earliest pioneers of globalisation. Today Muslim culture occupies a vast territory, from the Middle East to Asia, North Africa and South America, and is far from unitary. Yet it seems that the pluralism and dynamism of contemporary Muslim societies is being denied in the many recent buildings which have been festooned with geometrical shapes, domes and arches, *muqarnas*, minarets, *iwans*—all considered potent symbols of Muslim culture. Such stale and superficial gestures—a symptom of "paradigm paralysis"—neither respond to current conditions in Muslim society nor advance the art of building.

Symbols are frozen in time, acting as ready-made signs or images. Since the function of symbols is to recall a preexisting form or reality, they cannot express the culture of contemporary Muslim societies or in fact any other society, which are neither static nor confined geographically. In addition, the recognition of symbols depends on the presence of a shared cultural memory, and this can no longer be assumed in a pluralistic society. In classical architecture, for example, the proportions of the Doric column were seen as symbolic of an idealised male body. Given the homogeneity of ancient Greek society, the idea that the sensations emitted by the restrained aesthetic expression of the Doric column were commonly perceived as masculine, and also that any deviation from those proportions was an indication of weakness or femininity, is plausible. Today there is no consensus as to how forms are perceived, and symbols which once had the capacity to unite individuals in the public realm no longer have a cultural role. To evolve from a theatre of representation towards a theatre of movement, to retain the ability to register change, architecture must reject the use of symbolism.

Symbols continue to have a role in society, but they now occupy the realm of individual rather than collective affection. No built form is representational until it has been perceived as such by an individual, who, according to his or her experience, education or language, processes it into an affection and recognises it as a symbol of that experience. A form may produce a certain affection in one person but not in another, and become a symbol for one person but not for another.

If symbols can no longer coalesce their plural audience by providing them with a shared experience of their environment, then built forms are free to instigate their own ways of affecting individuals. Every built form possesses inherent affects and the ability to elicit specific sensations. An affect is a pre-personal intensity which enters into a dialogue with a human being—like a language that exists prior to words. Affects elicit different types of affections, such as moods, feelings, meanings or thoughts. Whereas affections are the effect of a form on an individual and are therefore subject to different types of mediation, affects are pre-personal and unmediated, and embed a form with the ability to be perceived in many ways. Through the agency of affects, built forms, like music, art, literature and films, are polysemous—producing different meanings. They therefore play a vital cultural role in contemporary society: They serve as a social fabric that allows individuals to share in the actuality of a form, but in a multiplicity of ways. To explore and develop architecture as a cultural practice, today's designers need to focus on the affects of buildings.

The resilience of the many great structures in Muslim societies that have survived is not based on what they once represented but on their ongoing affective performance. The Old Fatih mosque in Istanbul emits a unique mix of optical sensations of rotundity and asymmetry, and acoustic sensations of diffusion and slowness, which are due to its particular assemblage of domes. The Sukullu Mehmet Pasha mosque, also in Istanbul, emits sensations of rotundity, diffusion and slowness, but scalloping and symmetry as well. In the former the congregation would be oriented along the axis of asymmetry, whereas in the latter, with its symmetrical plan, it would be grouped in the centre. The Timcheh Amin al-Dowleh in the bazaar of Kashan, Iran, emits sensations of diamonding, cruciformity and gradation in addition to rotundity. The Sitt Zubaida mausoleum in Baghdad emits sensations of stepping and conicality as well as rotundity. The Sheikh Lotfollah mosque in Isfahan emits sensations of orthogonality, scalloping and granularity as well as rotundity. The affective differences between these structures are a consequence of the architects' search for novelty and difference.

In architecture, the pursuit of novelty is related to its cultural role, which is determined by the interaction between built forms and the public. This role is sustained by the way buildings function affectively rather than what they stand for, or their symbolic value. For architecture to contribute to the evolution of culture, architects need to produce forms that transmit novel affects. The Novel displaces the idea of the Old versus the New. Whereas symbols fundamentally conserve the old, or the existing, the New aims to bring about an abrupt and complete change, to achieve a foundational shift. Without such a shift, according to proponents of the New, culture remains static, unable to generate change and development. The Novel, on the other hand, acts within a given paradigm or culture by transforming what exists while repeating it. Each repetition changes the perception of the individuals that interact with the built form.

Successive repetitions together can produce significant change, a process that Thomas S. Kuhn described as "a quiet revolution".[1] The Novel therefore calls for ecological thinking, simultaneously embracing history and change. Each of the buildings mentioned above is based on the dome, yet no two use it in an identical way. The Old Fatih mosque repeats the surface dome asymmetrically and couples it with arches and pendentives. The Sukullu Mehmet Pasha mosque also repeats the surface dome, but in a symmetrical fashion, and couples it with arches and pendentives, producing four pockets of domed space and hence the additional sensation of scalloping. The Timcheh Amin al-Dowleh is a *yazdi-bandi* dome composed of horizontal tiers of quasi-pendentive surfaces spanning from an octagonal plan to a hexagonal top formed by a compression ring that also acts as an oculus. The Sitt Zubaida mausoleum adopts the *muqarnas* system of enclosing space, with the *muqarnas* arrayed along a circular plan and their diameters gradually diminishing in section, emitting a sensation of conicality. This use of the *muqarnas* differs from that of the Sheikh Lotfollah mosque, in which it is set above the arched entrance, embedded within a rectangular plan form, and framed by an arch. These examples show that the search for novelty in Muslim culture has generated a wide range of domes—surface dome, ribbed dome, *yazdi-bandi* dome, *kar-bandi* dome, *kaseh-sazi* dome, as well as the *muqarnas* dome—each expanding the art of building a dome as well as offering novel affects and sensations.

Our 21st-century environment is the product of diverse causes that emerge through multiple spheres—physical, mental and social—which are interlinked in complex ways. Accordingly, it presents us with enormous potential, as well as urgent concerns such as overconsumption, migration, climate change, urban sprawl, the decompression of the urban industrial city and the need for diversity in housing. To harness the potentials of contemporary reality for mobilising people into interacting with the built environment in new ways, architects need to engage with these processes of change and generate novel affects. The history of Muslim architecture offers innumerable examples of how architects can generate different novel forms with different affects. Out of the resulting plurality of experience will emerge the conditions in which divergent points of view can coexist, as well as a vital source of "essential tension" in architecture's pursuit of a critical cultural practice.[2]

Notes

1. In his book *The Structure of Scientific Revolutions*, Thomas S. Kuhn writes that Galileo's conjecture was merely that—a conjecture. So was Kepler's cosmology. But each conjecture increased the credibility of the other, and together they changed the prevailing perceptions of the scientific community. Later, Newton showed that Kepler's three laws could all be derived from a single theory of motion and planetary motion, thereby solidifying and unifying the paradigm shift that Galileo and Kepler had initiated. Thomas S. Kuhn, *The Structure of Scientific Revolutions* (Chicago: University of Chicago Press, 1962), chapter X, "Revolutions as Changes of World View", p. 111.

2. In *The Structure of Scientific Revolutions*, Thomas Kuhn argued that science is not a steady, cumulative acquisition of knowledge. Instead, science is a series of interludes, or "normal science", which are a consequence of scientists spending time addressing problems that are seen as puzzles, punctuated by "intellectually violent revolutions". These revolutions emerge as a result of the same puzzles being seen from another perspective, which act as a counter-instance and thus a source of crisis, leading to new ways of looking at those problems. Kuhn thereby argued that divergent points of view are an essential tension in any scientific research.

Walking Lightly on Earth
Souleymane Bachir Diagne

I had great expectations about learning a lot from my experience as a non-architect member of the Master Jury for the 2010 Aga Khan Award for Architecture. I had foreseen getting educated about architecture by my colleagues, given the good fortune of sitting with fellow jury members who are among the best in the world in that field, as well as in the related areas of landscape, design and art history. Little did I expect, however, to draw from the experience and from my interactions a new understanding of a wonderful philosophical novel that I have taught in my seminars on the history of philosophy in the Islamic world: Ibn Tufayl's Hayy ibn Yaqzan.

What made me think of that philosophic tale was a remark made from time to time by the chair of our jury, who would summarize everybody's reflections on the beauty, the efficiency and the message of a given building by saying that it "walked lightly on earth". That phrase is a reference to Quranic verses (25:63 to 77) in which "the true servants of the most Gracious" are described. What is said of them first and foremost is that they are "those who walk on the earth in humility" (or lightly). Obviously, when applied to architecture, the notion implies measurable parameters constitutive of the "footprint" of the project. But it certainly goes beyond those technical aspects. A building "walking lightly on earth" does not necessarily mean a "light" or "small" building: a skyscraper could perfectly qualify, as did a few magnificent "big" projects that were considered worthy of praise by the jury. Some of them have been shortlisted. Even a building that expands over the sea, provided the outreach is for good reasons, can qualify in the same way. What is meant then by light walking concerns generally the precision, the efficiency and the grace with which architectural works are produced, without waste or dross, in a way that manifests humility and respect for the earth.

The projects that ended up being shortlisted embody quite eminently that respect. One of them is the Tulou Collective Housing in Nanhai, China. Without being intrinsically "light", in terms of dimensions—because it has to respond to the necessity of providing low-income housing to a large population of migrant workers—it does give meaning to the multifaceted notion of light walking by its message and the example it offers. Inspired by fortress-like earth-houses designed to shelter and protect multiple families, known throughout the Fujian province as tulou, its message is one of reconciliation between the weight of necessity and the demand for light walking. In particular, tulou is a reminder, at the heart of fast-growing cities attracting more and more people away from their lands, that city buildings need not be the rupture with the rural worlds represented by repetitive and soulless housing projects weighing upon earth: on the contrary, they can be the reinvention, in new circumstances and situations, of the art of building from earth in a way that shows respect for the life of the community. To paraphrase Heidegger analysing "the origin of the work of art", it could be said here that the world created by the architectural work grounds itself on the earth while the earth juts through it.

One of the winners, the Ipekyol Textile Factory in Turkey, carries the same kind of message and adds another dimension to the meaning of light walking. Here is a country, Turkey, that by all accounts is one of the most dynamic economies in the world. An article from the New York Times (July 6, 2010) indicates that this "fast rising economic power", "with a core of internationally competitive companies turning the youthful nation into an entrepreneurial hub", currently enjoys 11.4 per cent growth—a rate "second only to China". When in such a country one of those "internationally competitive companies", in a sector unfortunately not known for good working conditions, decides to ask an architect to put the emphasis on the well-being of the employees, enabling them to "breathe" light in every spot within the factory, that is indeed another aspect of what it means to walk lightly on earth by showing respect for human labour. And the hope is, of course, that this project will set an example in the important domain of factory building.

The project that most embodies what it means to build "from the earth", and therefore to walk on it with humility, is certainly the Madinat al-Zahra Museum in Cordoba, Spain. The museum presents itself as literally coming out of earth, as the architects have chosen to keep it at the level of the archaeological site that it is designed to serve. Such an architectural choice, a physical translation of the organic link between museology and archaeology, reminds us of the etymological significance of humility: from the Latin humus, meaning earth. And it sends a powerful message that needs to be heard today: that Islam in Europe is one of its many roots, coming from its very soil. The museum, by burying itself, as it were, in the earth of Andalusia, stands as a reminder that the Muslim past of the region has been a nurturing element for Europe and is today an integral part of its identity. It belies the view of many who metonymically reduce Islam to minarets that they demonise as a symbol of both foreignness and arrogance. In so doing, it speaks of the past as well as the future of men and women who were, who are, fully European and fully Muslim.

In many ways Madinat al-Zahra carries such a message of respect, and its existence constitutes both a trace and a symbol of the civilisation of Andalusia that one scholar of medieval Spain, Maria Rosa Menocal, has beautifully called, in the title of her book on the unique culture of tolerance created in that land by the three Abrahamic religions, "the ornament of the world".

The evocation of Andalusia during the discussions of the Madinat al-Zahra Museum is probably what brought to my mind Ibn Tufayl and his Hayy Ibn Yaqzan and created the association between that philosophical work and the notion of walking lightly on earth.

Abu Bakr ibn Tufayl, who died in 1185 in Morocco, was born in Guadix, 50 miles northeast of Grenada. A master in philosophy and medicine, he served under the ruling Almohad dynasty as adviser, physician and friend of the sultan Abu Yaqub Yusuf. He was also a mentor for another famous Andalusian philosopher, Ibn Rushd, also known as Averroes, whom he introduced to the sultan. To demonstrate the Quranic notion of "fitra"—that is, an innate disposition to be enlightened with knowledge, in particular the knowledge of God, with which human beings are endowed—he chose the form of an allegorical novel. That novel tells the story of an infant, Hayy ibn Yaqzan (meaning: the Living, son of the Vigilant), abandoned on a desert island, raised by a gazelle, who grows up to develop to perfection all of the human capabilities in his nature and to become an enlightened sage, fully cognisant of the one God and of his own mission as a steward of His creation. It could be said without paradox that this allegory about a solitary figure is in fact a philosophical work on relationships. It is a book on self-education in essential connections: recognition of and connection with oneself; recognition of and connection with kindred beings or other selves; recognition of and connection with the divine; recognition of and connection with earth. All these connections are manifestations of the cosmic driving force of love, which he first tasted as an infant and a little boy in the bond with his deer-mother.

It takes many stages for Hayy to comprehend all of these connections and his place in a totality held together by love. After a phase of violence and arrogance, during which he would perform vivisection on animals to try to understand the very principle of life and the significance of death, he gradually comes to understand that it is his most fundamental duty vis-à-vis earth and the life it nurtures to protect it, expand it, enlighten it: that is what stewardship of the earth commands. In other words, he comes to understand what it means to inhabit the world, and not think of himself as its master and possessor. It is in that sense that Hayy ibn Yaqzan deserves a prominent place in the history of works devoted to ecological awareness.

Nothing is said in the tale about the buildings that this Robinson Crusoe avant la lettre creates on his island. But it is obvious, from the trajectory that led him to fully realise who he was meant to be, that his architecture will be inspired by his preoccupation with the meaning of inhabiting. One could have in mind—I had—the likes of the Green School, one of the projects shortlisted, a sustainable campus where everything is made of bamboo and where the students are taught, primarily, to have a passion for Planet Earth. Other projects that are not buildings translate as well the notion of inhabiting earth: the Wadi Hanifa Wetlands that breathed life back into the environment near Riyadh, the project in Tunis designed to revitalise the colonial heritage of the city along with that of its "medina", etc.—are all examples of Hayy's architecture, the art of walking lightly on earth.

Note
1. Maria Rosa Menocal, *The Ornament of the World: How Muslims, Jews and Christians Created a Culture of Tolerance in Medieval Spain* (New York, Boston, London: Little, Brown and Company, 2002).

Hope
Alice Rawsthorn

When the historians of the future look back at this time, what will they see? Environmental crisis? Economic recession? Social instability? Political turbulence? Intellectual neurosis? No doubt. As for the consequences? War? Poverty? Terrorism? Pandemics? Rising crime? Ecological disasters? Mass unemployment? Social unrest? Probably.

One can only hope that the same historians will also note the courageous efforts to combat these problems. The five winners of the 2010 Cycle of the Aga Khan Award for Architecture are inspired and inspiring examples of attempts to forge solutions to complex challenges faced not only by the Muslim world but by people everywhere. Though these projects—a wetland, a factory, a school, a historic area of a city and a museum—are dramatically different in their scale and objectives, each offers hope to people who desperately need it.

One of the five is not only a model of ecological infrastructure but addresses the human problems posed by urbanisation, which is accelerating so aggressively that over half of the global population now live in cities for the first time in history, making those cities ever bigger, denser, more crowded, polluted and threatening. The Wadi Hanifa Wetlands has created a pleasant, safe and tranquil public space for the people of Riyadh within easy reach of a city where such places are so scarce that families are forced to picnic on the sidewalks.

Urbanisation is invariably the consequence of industrialisation, which causes another problem: the poor quality of workplaces, particularly factories in developing economies, where many millions of people work in unsavoury, sometimes dangerous conditions. An enlightened exception is the Ipekyol Textile Factory in the Turkish city of Edirne, a clean, congenial workplace where providing decent conditions for the workers is seen as making an important contribution to the increasing efficiency and profitability of the business.

Yet another problem arising from urbanisation is the escalation of rural poverty, particularly in developing countries where many millions of people are fleeing the countryside in search of employment in towns and cities. As rural populations dwindle, local resources such as schools, shops and medical centers are forced to close, prompting yet more people to leave. The Bridge School in the Chinese village of Xiashi has revitalised a declining rural community by literally bridging the creek that has divided it historically to create an engaging place for local children to fulfil their learning potential.

Navigating the new—whether in the form of a public space, a workplace or a school—is one challenge of modern life; dealing with the old can be equally problematic, not least when it evokes a painful period of history. The restoration of the late 19th- and early 20th-century colonial buildings in the Bab B'Har district of Tunis addresses this adroitly. By using architectural restoration to nurture new skills and commercial opportunities, it has regenerated the local economy in an unusually sensitive reading of Tunisia's colonial history.

Equally sensitive is the design of the Madinat al-Zahra Museum near the Spanish city of Cordoba, where the public can appreciate and learn from the excavation of one of the world's most important early Islamic archaeological sites. It has done so by creating a graceful and expressive building, which sits so lightly on the landscape that it acts as a physical symbol of tolerance and empathy. Like the other four projects, it is an architectural expression of hope.

Chairman's Award

Oleg Grabar
Chairman's Award Citation

The Aga Khan Award for Architecture's fourth Chairman's Award is given to Oleg Grabar, distinguished scholar and teacher, in acknowledgment of the valuable contributions he has made to studying the Islamic world's architectural evolution, from the early Islamic period to the present. Through his teaching, writings and lectures, Oleg Grabar has greatly widened and enriched our understanding of the Islamic world's architectural production, emphasising its geographic and chronological diversity, as well as positioning it within its wider political, social, cultural and economic contexts.

Oleg Grabar has done more to define the field of Islamic art and architecture than almost anyone else alive. The questions he has asked, the hypotheses he has proposed and the theories he has developed, over a career that now spans more than six decades, have shaped and defined the way we understand the Islamic world's rich architectural heritage.

Grabar's work is as broad as it is incisive. He has written seminal studies about Islam's earliest monuments as well as some of its most recent ones, his interests ranging from North Africa and Spain to Iran and India. His work on the Dome of the Rock in Jerusalem, the Great Mosque of Isfahan and the Allhambra in Granada, to name but three of his more than thirty books, are standards in the field and reveal his ability to work across cultures and time. His 1973 publication, *The Formation of Islamic Art*, remains one of the most lucid and insightful investigations of the emerging culture of the new faith ever written.

Although trained as an art historian, Grabar is above all a cultural historian. From the outset his work crossed disciplines using architectural history, anthropology, archaeology, literary criticism, linguistics, semiotics and philology, among others, to enrich and illuminate our understanding of the art and architecture of the Islamic world. His goal throughout has been the same: to bring to life the buildings and objects that so interest him, and through them to explore the social, political and cultural context of the people who made and used them. He has approached this task with an extraordinary generosity of spirit, an endless curiosity and a consistent interest in the latest issues and questions.

Grabar has often stated that he is less interested in answers than he is in raising questions. As a result his work, while often definitive, is first and foremost an invitation to join him on a journey of intellectual discovery as he speculates on a wide range of issues, from early

Umayyad architecture to the latest buildings in the United Arab Emirates, from how the Ottomans and Safavids used the built environment to articulate their political agendas, to how contemporary societies define themselves through architecture.

In 1981, Grabar was instrumental in establishing, with His Highness the Aga Khan and William Porter, the joint programme in Islamic Art and Architecture at Harvard University and MIT, and was one of the founding members of the Steering Committee of the Aga Khan Award for Architecture in 1976. He has also served on the jury of the Aga Khan Award for Architecture and written extensively for the Award's many publications.

For all of Grabar's renown as a scholar and advocate for the importance of Islamic art and architecture, his greatest legacy may be as an educator who has taught hundreds if not thousands of students, first at the University of Michigan and then at Harvard University. Many of these students have gone on to become respected scholars, educators, curators, architects and public officials, and they are a living testimony to Grabar's fascination with the art and architecture of the Islamic world.

Scholar, teacher, intellectual and historian, Oleg Grabar has devoted his life to trying to understand and explain the complex forces that gave rise to an artistic tradition that now spans fourteen centuries. No one has done so with more aplomb and insight.

Oleg Grabar's Other Biography
Mohammad al-Asad

In 1976, Oleg Grabar, a Harvard professor, was invited to lunch with two people he had not met before: William Porter, Dean of the School of Architecture and Planning at the Massachusetts Institute of Technology (MIT), and Boston-based landscape architect Garr Campbell. They asked Grabar if he would be interested in joining a small group that would advise His Highness the Aga Khan on a project involving past and current architecture in Islamic lands.

Soon afterward, the three met with the Aga Khan and a few of his staff, as well as a small group of architects including Sir Hugh Casson from Britain and Charles Correa from India. That meeting led to the creation of the Aga Khan Award for Architecture. Oleg Grabar was a member of its first Steering Committee, and he continued to be actively involved with the Award for many years.

A few years later, the Aga Khan held another meeting with Grabar and Porter. He expressed an interest in establishing a joint programme at their respective institutions devoted to studying the Islamic world's built environment. This meeting led to another that included the presidents of the two universities, and soon afterward the Aga Khan Program for Islamic Architecture at Harvard and MIT was created. Both the Award and the Program have had a marked influence during the last three decades on the study and practice of architecture and urbanism connected to Muslim communities.

This account is provided by Oleg Grabar in the introduction to the third volume of his collected essays, Constructing the Study of Islamic Art: Islamic Art and Beyond. The recollection points to another aspect of Grabar's well-known intellectual curiosity. He has been a prolific writer on the Islamic world's visual culture, as the partial list of his many publications provided in his curriculum vitae attests. But he also has been reflecting on how the study of this visual culture has evolved over the half century since he became involved with it. This historiographic interest is not at all surprising to those who have known Grabar.

It is a theme he has been frequently but informally discussing with colleagues for some time. Recently, however, he has started to lecture and publish on it.

Grabar's reflections on the development of the study of the Islamic world's visual culture are very valuable. Not only do they present the ruminations of a highly inquisitive and perceptive mind, they include the accounts of a figure who has been at the centre of this development, and often an instrumental force in shaping it.

In reflecting on the significance of the Aga Khan Award for Architecture, Grabar discusses how it has brought together worlds that previously had operated independently. The Award has brought academia into contact with the "real world", a world greatly influenced by financial, economic and political decision makers rather than researchers and educators. It has also brought scholars who had studied only the Islamic world's past into contact with its present, and with parts they had not studied before and knew very little about. These encounters, with their effects of cross-fertilisation, are still unfolding and are having a profound impact on the field as a whole.

For Grabar himself, these new investigations have been transformative. They introduced him to an aspect of the Islamic world that is considerably different from what he had come to know. Before these exchanges, his contact with the Islamic world had been primarily through texts and objects, or through limited but more direct interactions with the people of the land through excavations in the Syrian steppe or sojourns in cities of the Middle East such as Jerusalem, Damascus, Beirut and Cairo.

Such encounters that the Aga Khan Award and the Aga Khan Program brought about between the worlds of academia and events taking place on the ground today define one moment in the field's development that Grabar articulates. He also identifies other important moments. He takes us back to the field of Islamic art and architecture he entered when he began his career during the 1950s as a young man in his early 20s. Academically as well as intellectually, it then was defined by the param eters of the disciplines of medieval art and the art of late antiquity. The interests of those investigating it were limited to the formative centuries of Islam, particularly the first two. They rarely ventured beyond AD 1500, let alone into the modern period. Important artistic and architectural traditions such as those of the Ottomans, Safavids or Mughals were given scant attention.

Outside of academia, the field also was being formed by a fascinating world consisting primarily of collectors and travelers. These individuals were more daring in exploring the field's frontiers than their more conservative academic counterparts, examining periods, geographies and works that academia shied away from. Collectors provide a particularly interesting chapter in the evolution of the study of Islamic art. Although many of them had an incredibly refined sense of the visual, there were serious limitations to the contributions they could make to the field. Their world revolved around money more than scholarship. In contrast to the world of scholarship, it emphasised secrecy, particularly regarding who owned what and how much they paid for it, rather than disseminating information. Moreover, the financial rewards it offered attracted a few disreputable figures, some of whom were not above smuggling works of art or even stealing them.

Grabar also describes a field that was completely dominated by Western institutions. This was particularly evident in the Middle East. These institutions included Western universities as well as archaeological centres in the Middle East that were run by Western governments or private learned societies, primarily British, French and American—that is, the victors of World War II. These countries exercised tremendous political, military and economic clout, if not outright control, over many parts of the Islamic world. They had almost unrestricted access to historical works and sites. Such influence was further strengthened by the serious interest in history and archaeology exhibited by many of their diplomats stationed in the Middle East. The study of the Islamic world was thereby closely connected to Western imperialism and, in certain instances, to colonialism.

This Western domination has become somewhat diluted today, as a considerable number of universities and research centres have come into being in the Islamic world, producing their own educators and researchers. It also has been challenged in the postcolonial period by rising political tensions between a number of Muslim and Western governments. These tensions limit the access of Westerners to sites and also push local researchers to develop their own narratives independent of, and sometimes in isolation from, the West. Still, domination of the West over the field has not yet been undermined.

This leads to the subject of Orientalism, a term that Grabar feels has received some unfair critique. Orientalists studying the Islamic world's built environment included archaeologists who looked at their profession in what Grabar describes as "the richest and widest ways" period. Among those, he cites Ernst Herzfeld and Jean Sauvaget as notable figures, both active during the first half of the 20th century. There also were architects who became historians as they studied buildings they encountered in new lands, even though they did not originally set out with such intentions. Among those, Grabar identifies Pascal Coste, Max Herz and K.A.C. Creswell. These three made very important contributions to studying the architectural heritage of Islamic Cairo over the course of the 19th and 20th centuries. Such figures put together a wealth of information on the Islamic world's architectural heritage. Grabar, however, also points out that while these scholars devoted their careers to studying the Islamic world's past, they often showed little interest in its contemporary life.

Grabar reflects on how the state of affairs that had materialised during the period of European imperialism began to undergo drastic changes in the 1960s and 1970s. To begin with, as in any growing field, the study of Islamic art and architecture has expanded significantly to include new periods, regions and types of works. Moreover, in the West, a younger generation of academics rebelled against the "old boy network" prevalent in universities, demanding an end to the exclusion of disenfranchised groups such as women and minorities. Also important was a new emphasis on "relevance" that challenged the more narrowly defined and detached scholarly traditions.

The attacks on Orientalism succeeded in transforming what had been a highly respected field of inquiry into one with pejorative overtones. Here, Grabar cites the primary role that the late Palestinian-American literary critic and academic Edward Said played beginning in the 1970s in mounting a devastating critique of Orientalism through what Grabar identifies as a "brilliant gesture of anger". Said was among the growing voices that insisted that the people of the Islamic world become more actively engaged in the study of their past. As Grabar often points out, until only two decades ago, most students in American universities studying Islamic art and architecture were Western. Today the majority are from Muslim lands. As these various shifts take place, the methodological frameworks defining our overall understanding of the Islamic heritage are bound to undergo corresponding transformations.

These are tumultuous times characterised by overwhelming change and instability. The evolution of the study of Islamic art and architecture has expressed these changes, though in a quieter and slower manner than the social, economic and political transformations themselves. Changes affecting the field have included an added emphasis on how the visual world can function as an expression of identity. They also have included a glaring and often uncomfortable juxtapositioning of studying the "Other" and studying the "Self", and a rising tension between attempting to put forward a dispassionate study of the past and an engaged one that emphasises relevance to the present. These are all questions to which Oleg Grabar has been giving increased attention during recent years.

Notes

1. See Oleg Grabar, *Constructing the Study of Islamic Art*, 4 vols. (London: Ashgate, 2005–2006). The publication is also available online at: http://archnet.org/library/documents/collection.jsp?collection_id=1563.
2. See also Mohammad al-Asad and Majd Musa, "Half a Century in the Study of Islamic Art: An Essay on a Presentation Made by Oleg Grabar", in Mohammad al-Asad and Majd Musa, eds., *Exploring the Built Environment: Essays on the Presentations of Diwan al-Mimar and Affiliated Public Lectures* (Amman: Center for the Study of the Built Environment and Darat al Funun—The Khalid Shoman Foundation, 2007), pp. 13–30. The publication is also available online at: http://www.csbe.org/e_publications/islamic_art/islamic_art.htm. Both online publications cited in this essay were accessed in July 2010.

On Knowledge and Education
Oleg Grabar

Some 35 years ago, when I had the honour and pleasure to help His Highness the Aga Khan design the first steps of what was then simply the Aga Khan Award for Architecture—now an enormous enterprise operating on five continents and affecting the lives and welfare of many people—his dream for the growth and development of the environment of Muslims, wherever they live and work, was already fully present in spirit, if not yet organised in the flesh. Two questions dominated our discussions then: Is there a cultural phenomenon rightly called Islamic architecture, and how do we find out what it is? And once we learn what it is, how do we let the world in general and Muslim communities in particular know what it is (or was) in order to maintain its quality and presumed uniqueness, while supporting its practitioners in bringing it up to the most effective economic and cultural practices of our own day? In other words, we were supposed to acquire knowledge and provide a programme of education.

In a sense, our task of many years back can be justified by an often quoted Tradition (hadith) attributed to the Prophet Muhammad that knowledge must be sought wherever it is found, even in China. China in the 7th century of the common era and the first century of the hijrah was a way to identify a remote world known to exist and to be important, though hardly accessible. The point of the Tradition is that there is knowledge everywhere, none of which should be rejected. Both of these implications are still pertinent today. Knowledge is indeed created everywhere, and China has become a central actor in the cultural as well as economic realms of today's world. What has changed dramatically since the time of the Prophet and keeps changing in ways which are almost impossible to predict are the nature of knowledge and the means in our possession to deal with it.

Such contemporary comments on the hadith as are known to me do not talk about education. At the time of the Prophet, transmission of knowledge was relatively simple, through writing, copying and reading books and through oral arguments kept in the memories of participants. Any intelligent person was then able to master much of what was known. The breadth of knowledge within any one talented individual before the 17th century can at times be truly breathtaking. Education was one with knowledge and took place wherever there was a library and a few literate and concerned individuals.

Today's scene is dramatically different. There are as many centres producing knowledge as there are countries and universities, technical schools, archaeological institutes, hospitals or museums. Much of this knowledge is available in what I once counted as 30 different languages (I am sure it is many more now). It exists in millions of books, hundreds of journals, thousands of reports, and now, thanks to the Internet and Google, this knowledge is accessible, in theory at least, almost everywhere in the world. Museum collections have been photographed and recorded, exhibitions preserved forever on DVD's. And I suppose that architectural firms and excavators preserve whatever they find and do on masses of disks. In short, the quantity of available information is enormous, so large that it cannot be mastered. No one can say anymore that he knows all about Islamic art, about the architectural projects of today, about excavations or about objects from any one period of history.

This explosion of knowledge has by necessity led to either one of two positions. One is to limit one's competence and claim knowledge in only narrowly defined spheres—the Ottoman world of the 18th century, the ceramics of Iran, or the contribution of Hassan Fathy to contemporary architecture in the Islamic world. Specialisation becomes the order given to knowledge, and it tends to be determined by the narrow restrictions provided by limited linguistic competence or area awareness. Specialisation tends to become national and linguistically limited, but it presumes thoroughness and completeness in whatever one's area may be. It also requires large numbers of equally competent specialists who may or may not find ways of communicating with each other.

The other position was outlined to me some years ago by an early Internet activist with concerns in the natural sciences. He indicated that every week I could receive automatically, as in a newsletter or by email, a summary in English and with illustrations of every newly published piece of information within the history of Islamic art or the practice of contemporary architects. This survey would include a judgment as to the significance and value of that information, wherever it appeared and in whatever language it was presented. According to this position, what an explosion of knowledge needs is, first of all, the formation of a class of intermediary consultants who channel information and evaluate it for use by others, guaranteeing the accuracy of what they relate and its appropriateness to whatever we need and already know. To some degree, for our broad area of the man-made environment of the Islamic world, this consulting function can be fulfilled by the online databank ArchNet, a creation of the Aga Khan Trust for Culture and MIT. But I am not sure that ArchNet is capable of reacting rapidly to new knowledge and distributing its awareness to all of its constituents. Part of my uncertainty derives from the absence of broad categories of understanding architecture which would automatically be known to all and which would always be consistently included in all new information.

A simple example of such category is that of the material of construction: stone, brick, concrete and so forth. But there are much more complex categories of understanding which are either, like style, impossible to define, or like design, too difficult to explain in theory, if not in practice. Finally, although the means exist to make knowledge of architecture available, this is not true of the other arts, where utter disorder of knowledge is still the rule. But it is not simply a matter of establishing categories of description and understanding. It is also a matter of making these categories enter the cognitive mind of people and groups. This is how I understand the purposes and requirements of education.

Education can and should be understood at three different levels. The first level is the scholarly one, the level of the learned practitioner. It is the highest one because its aim extends beyond the acquisition of knowledge to the creation of further knowledge. But it is also the easiest one to handle and understand. Naturally and professionally, it is centred on maximum information and the development of ideas. It is restricted only by the linguistic limitations of its practitioners and the time available to deal with it. The development of a category of consultants, as outlined above, and constant improvements in the operation of the Internet should take care of its needs and lead to scholarship that would constantly improve the field of learning and be made available through the usual mechanisms of higher education such as seminars, colloquia and publication in books and periodicals of specialised interest.

The second level can be called the level of social leadership. It involves those people and institutions that are, or seem to be, running governments and financial or industrial enterprises and defining the cultural context of their actions. They make decisions about school curricula and university programmes, sponsor films and television programmes, publish newspapers and magazines. The forms of government in which they operate may vary a great deal, and in their hands lies something more important than the sponsorship of activities or the interplay of politics. They provide rewards and awards, they accept or reject the implications of new investments—whether an airport, a university or the restoration of a historic building. They decide whether something is going to be characterised as Islamic, Arab or Egyptian, and they define the features to be used in preparing urban developments or in the behaviour and vocabulary of diplomats and educators. They accept or change symbols—flags, occasionally clothes or simply colours—credibly associated with a land or a culture. Although it is easy enough to identify the aims and ambitions of this level of education, it is more difficult to describe the ways in which it can be enriched. One wants to avoid the policing of thought or the creation of compulsory national, ethnic or religious sets of forms and doctrines, but how does one maintain a climate of appropriate openness for many available forms of knowledge to ensure that one's world reflects its traditions, even in its modernity, without becoming absurdly self-centric or entirely transformed by foreign imports?

The third level of education lies with the mass of the population. There are many myths and falsehoods in the collective memory of large and small groups of people. These can be dangerous and lead to the destruction of monuments or sites, the assassination of opponents, or, on a less upsetting level, the broadcasting of false slogans or the sponsorship of dubious causes. At this stage of thinking about a topic removed from my area of knowledge and competence, I would argue that public education must concentrate on the media shared by all, such as radio, film and television, and on the primary and secondary schools attended by all boys and girls. The enlightenment and training of primary and secondary school teachers seems to me essential, because they ultimately fashion the beliefs, attitudes and eventually passions of all men and women.

My first level, that of scholarly knowledge and education, is fairly clear and requires only important technical components to be successful. The development of university-level academics, of teachers and thinkers in professional schools and of well-established practitioners, can be achieved with a minimum of effort, once certain mechanisms of information and judgement are developed and the gap lessened between wealthy and poor countries. Matters are more complicated when we deal with education for leaders and for the general public. The Aga Khan Award for Architecture and its several related activities are, to my knowledge, the only organisations which have tried to reach publics that are so different from the professionals of architecture.

Education, like high scholarship and sophisticated knowledge, is a nonstop activity operating day and night and already affecting the leaders of tomorrow. It requires constant attention and a continuing commitment at all levels, and especially at my second and third levels, if the beautiful dreams vaguely defined some 35 years ago can become living realities.

The Role of the Historian*
Oleg Grabar

More than once over the years, and especially after the creation of the Aga Khan Program in Islamic Architecture at Harvard and MIT, and during my many years on the Steering Committee of the Aga Khan Award for Architecture, the question had arisen in my mind on the role and usefulness of the historian within the aims and activities of those professionals—architects, planners, economists, decision makers of all sorts—who are building the future.

Within universities, a historical component is a normal and accepted part of an academic programme, even if the reasons for this acceptance have not always been thought out. What follows then is an attempt to set down some ideas about the values of historical knowledge for discussion by those other than historians or simply as a cathartic exercise, for much is troubling me when I see how misused and misunderstood the past is within the Muslim world. It is well at the very beginning to recall, however, that the issue is not a Muslim one alone. Italian and German fascism were anchored in certain visions of history, and Marxism began with a theory of history that had almost destroyed Russian historical scholarship. But it is not necessary to go to these extremes. All national movements, all nationalisms (the new American right, Corsicans, Basques, Irish, Ukrainians) involve history as some sort of justification. At Trinity College in Dublin, half of the history courses have dealt with Irish history, and none with anything south of the Mediterranean or east of Germany. What these samples mean is that a knowledge of history is not simply a form of culture, like good table manners, it is an instrument in that search for identity, in that pride of one's own world, of one's own past, which concerns political and cultural leaders as well as educational and intellectual ones. History, even the history of architecture, is not a neutral subject, but an active one that can be explosive.

What follows consists only of thoughts for discussion and reflection. I have taken somewhat extreme positions on a few issues, partly to provoke discussion and partly to protect the integrity of what I see more and more as separate activities: understanding what happened, doing something today, and being one's self.

Can one define History? It is perhaps easier to define the tasks of the historian. There are four fundamental historical tasks. Although the best historians can perform all four, these tasks do not require the same aptitudes and technical equipment, and, for the most part, every historian tends to be better qualified for one of them than for the others.

The first task is that of defining moments of time and space and of identifying the unique characteristics of each such moment. A priori, this is a most objective task. Its questions, limited to architecture, are of two kinds: 1) broad and synthetic: What was the visually perceptible configuration of Cairo, Istanbul or Delhi in 1550? 2) concrete and restricted: It being known that the mosque of Damascus was completed between 705 and 715, what did it look like at that time, what meanings were attributed to it, what techniques or decorations were used in it?

The equipment necessary for the successful achievement of these aims are: the archaeology of a time or of a building, that is, the carefully documented reconstruction of an artefact in a stated and fixed chronological sequence; contemporary or otherwise valid literary sources ranging from inscriptions to descriptions; an awareness of the contemporary ethos through chronicles and literature as well as political and social events. The central concern of this task is as absolute a synchrony as possible. Its ideals are the exact reconstruction of a building, a complete explanation of why it was built, and the reaction of the first person who saw it. Its primary sin is anachronism, that is, attributing motifs and attitudes that cannot be of that time or of that place. Its methodological difficulty is that, since the historian of today is the product of his time and not of the time he describes, he is never free of his ideological constraints and tends to interpret sources according to his ethos. For instance, my own interpretations of the Dome of the Rock could not have been reached without the Cold War in which I was brought up as a young

adult. Did I read in the texts of the time something of my own time? Or could I understand that monument because its period was similar to mine? The ambiguities of this "objective" history, "as it happened" in the words of Leopold von Ranke, can only be removed if the historian moves away from his subject and only serves as a warrantor of authenticity. He separates that which is original from that which is reconstructed, he measures and describes, but he does not explain unless he has contemporary sources to do so. Let me call this historian the antiquarian. His heart is usually quite pure in the sense that he is genuinely concerned for the truth of the past and that he is minimally affected by emotional or other relationships to that past. But is he of any more use to the world of today than a detective in a novel solving murders that were never committed?

Let me give an example. A first-rate antiquarian book is R. W. Hamilton's *The Structural History of the Aqsa Mosque* (London, 1949). Its 100-odd pages are very difficult to read, as one flips from text to drawings to illustrations, and it explains in unbearable detail based on shapes of stones or fragments of plaster the evolution of one of the great mosques of Islam. It is as nearly perfect as a scientific book can be, even if one can quibble as to whether his Aqsa I and Aqsa II are 8th- and 9th-century buildings or 7th and 8th. But never in this book is there a sense of why the mosque is important, of what led to its erection, of why it was changed so often, and so on. It is a perfect book and yet is hardly ever read and is not found in most bibliographies or most libraries in the world. The "real" truth it depicts seems to be of no interest.

The second type of historian is the diachronist or diatopist. He has studied the works of antiquarians and is trying to extract from them such themes, ideas, attitudes or whatever that seems to him to cut across centuries or areas. It could be the search for constants (a certain type of space usable for large crowds to gather leads him from Roman fora to mosques and to football stadiums), for changes and evolution (the development of the dome), for types of life or behaviour (the history of the palace or of urban piety), for regional characteristics (Anatolian-Ottoman construction practices), for a broad cut across areas (architecture around 1000 or 1500), or for the meaning of forms (the symbolism of the minaret, the structure of the Muslim city). In theory at least, the practitioner of this type of history must possess all of the technical skills of the antiquarian (often increased linguistically because of different areas and times) and, in addition, two supplementary talents. One is a theoretical skill that allows him to use terms like "symbol", "squinch", "ornament" or "space" in ways that are meaningful beyond the restricted field of Islamic architecture. The other is an ability to choose topics that are significant. A very learned and thorough study by an Egyptian scholar of many years ago on the calyx in ornament throughout the centuries is hardly pertinent to any known important issue, even though accompanied by thousands of wonderful drawings. On the other hand, several recent and older books (by authors including Prisse d'Avennes, Jules Bourgoin, Issam al-Said and Keith Critchlow) on geometric ornament in architecture and elsewhere deal with major issues but are so insufficiently antiquarian as to lose most of their value.

The problem, it seems to me, is that a diachronic or a diatopical approach makes two intellectual or ideological presuppositions. One is that there are threads which tie together certain times, cultural entities, areas and social-economic conditions. Here are a few examples: Whatever influences have come to bear on Syria, they were nearly always translated into stone, whereas Egypt had throughout its history a much more complex interplay between stone and brick, and Iran hardly knew stone at all. The Ottoman Empire developed a type of dome-centered mosque that became as much a place of worship as the symbol of Ottoman presence. In the 7th through 10th centuries, very different areas acquired a fairly common Islamic culture that justifies understanding its monuments as one entity, regardless of regional details. There accordingly is an acceptable ideological parallel between the Alhambra, the Topkapi Seray, the Kremlin, Versailles and the Red Fort in Lahore, because they are all products of princely patronage. There also is an architecture of domes that is only secondarily dependent on the cultures that created it;

and so forth. As one can see, these threads are, if one is just to use this approach, of many different types, and their proper elaboration requires a breadth of knowledge and experience that extends much beyond a given culture, period or area. Hence the study of such threads has easily become superficial or has sought help in pre-established abstract doctrines like functionalism, Marxism, technologism, regionalism, evolutionism and whatever else the social sciences can invent. I should add that while such approaches to history are easy enough to illustrate for Western architecture (as in the writings of Nikolaus Pevsner, Sigfried Gideon, Bruno Zevi, Eugène Emmanuel Viollet-le-Duc or Banister Fletcher), they are very rare in Islamic art (with some exceptions for regionalism) where superficiality predominates, at least in the grand manuals or general surveys. The reason is that most writers on these subjects do not have a deep feeling for the variants of Islamic culture.

The second presupposition of the diachronist and, perhaps to a smaller degree, diatopist is that his conclusions and paradigms have a continuing validity up to the present time and into the future. In other words, the definitions of regional style, of culturally identifiable ways of building, are not supposed to be simply definitions of a past but expressions of a permanent identity, one could almost say a gestalt, of carefully circumscribed cultural entities. The point was characteristic of Soviet scholarship in which the emphasis on Azari, Uzbek, Turkmen or Tajik traditions up to this day permeates all but antiquarian writing. But certainly Iranian, Egyptian or Turkish works have not escaped the assumption that somehow their millenary past has lessons to offer to today, and it is the historian's role to identify, as carefully and as scientifically as possible, whatever visual systems or meanings from the past are still pertinent. It is legitimate to ask of the historian what are the continuities of any one area. What may not be right is to assume that whatever remains is part of that continuity.

This second approach of the historian is obviously far more rewarding than the first one. It makes an impact on the outside world; it connects Islamic culture with world culture; it provides ideas and slogans to contemporary practitioners and political leaders; it eliminates immanent peculiarities and idiosyncrasies; and it extracts from monuments their wider and more abstract or paradigmatic significance. Its problems are, first of all, accuracy, but in a deeper sense, it is veracity and more specifically cultural veracity. This is a very important point on which I would like to elaborate. It is easy enough for any trained and sensitive historian to see in a sequence of forms (for instance, the large hypostyle mosque from Damascus to Delhi) a series of changes within a consistent concern for the creation of a large space for the Muslim community. And it is equally easy for an eloquent or articulate writer to derive from these changes an open-ended linear progression from a historical tradition into the future (for instance, the notion that complex geometric designs are necessary means for composing and decorating a building).

The problem lies precisely in the step that extrapolates from the past to the present and future. It is a temptation that is difficult to resist, perhaps even impossible to resist, but it is essential for the historian to stop his interpretation at the moment when a living culture appears. In my view, he must stop—as a historian, even if he belongs to the culture (he can obviously go on as a citizen of the culture, or as a member of the Ummah, the community of the faithful, but not as a historian). And, if he is not a Muslim, he cannot go beyond yet another point. It would be nice if, like the boundaries of the Arabian sanctuaries, this point could be neatly defined. In reality, it is not and I have often over the years tried to imagine where lies that invisible line beyond which only those who belong can go. Or should such a line exist in the 21st century, when everything physical can be seen from a satellite?

I can be much briefer on a third type of historian, the chronicler. The chronicler is the observer of an activity who records it in its minutest details. I do not know of a chronicler of a building or of an architect in classical or medieval times. The closest examples would be someone like Abbot Sugar from the 12th century recording his own activity at St. Denis, or a few passages from the writings of the Persian historian

Rashid al-Din (d. 1318) or the founder of the Mughal dynasty Babur (d. 1530). Perhaps a Maqrizi describing 15th-century Cairo comes closest to the kind of descriptive and interpretive statement found in a Joinville describing St. Louis in the 13th century, Suetonius or Tacitus writing about Roman emperors, or the 16th-century Ayn-i Akbar document describing the administration of the Mughal emperor Akbar. We know that there were no Vasari in the Middle Ages, and I am not sufficiently familiar with literature after 1500 to be sure that chroniclers of architecture did not exist. They certainly can exist for the contemporary world, and, just as no architect can survive today without a good photographer, every architect should perhaps add to his staff a chronicler. Like a photographer, the chronicler can enhance or damage the work created, but he can never create it himself. In part, the role of the chronicler has been taken in the contemporary world by the critic, but I wonder whether the ideal critic does not, in theory at least, choose his subjects, whatever the reasons for the choice, rather than being selected by a creator to record something. But I am willing to stand corrected on this point by those who have more experience with criticism. Thus while I maintain the importance of a historian-chronicler as a type, I am not sure that he exists as yet in the flesh.

Finally there is the "new" historian who has grown most spectacularly in French circles over the past twenty years. He deals either with issues that are so broad (the nature of brick or the geometry of space) that they are not culturally significant, or with the elaboration of the specific to the point where it loses its diachronic value. (I know of no appropriate example in the History of Art, but there are many in literature, or in economic history; a partial and not very successful example could be my own treatment of the Alhambra (Cambridge, MA, 1978), which in some ways defined the building as a type, not as a monument). This kind of history almost rejects a priori the cultural concerns that are ours.

Of my four types of historians, the chronicler is only useful to the contemporary world if he can provide adequate documentation about contemporary practices and set it down in such a way that it can be of use to other contemporary critics, historians and practitioners, or else if he can provide information for the antiquarian or diachronist of the future. The antiquarian is only useful, in fact essential, for restorations and reconstructions. It is an important activity frequently proclaimed in official pronouncements all over the world. I have developed a lot of reservations about the ways in which it has been implemented in practice and argued in theory. I wonder, for instance, whether reconstructions and restorations are not always an admission that something had died. But death is the normal end for people and for buildings. Then why mummify buildings and not people? Otherwise, the antiquarian's value is limited, because his objective is always to explain a moment or a monument in the past, in its own time. He confuses issues by pointing out that concepts of today may have been meaningless in the past and, so very often, that the monument we see is not the one that was. The general theorist is only interesting for ideas and formulas.

We are left, then only with the diachronist or diatopist, and especially the former, as the kind of historian who seems to be useful for the contemporary world. But this is exactly where he has failed most conspicuously in dealing with Islamic art, where he has in fact even been destructive. The reason is, I think, a simple one. Whereas most major Western historians of this type began with a concern with contemporary, or, at the very least, modern architecture, their counterparts dealing with the Islamic world began as medievalists and antiquarians and then, through interest or seduction, moved on to more recent times. But their roots, their real expertise, were always in a remote past. They are the ones who defined "Islamic" architectural and aesthetic values through a small number of preserved major monuments of the past rather than through 90 per cent of the architectural setting of Islamic lands that was created in the 19th and 20th centuries.

They created the paradoxes with which we live: an aesthetic ideal and a sense of achievement earlier than the time of the actual visual experience and visual literacy of the contemporary Muslim world.

It thus becomes possible to suggest that, at this stage of intellectual effort, it may be more useful to forget about the past, to leave it to antiquarians. For the present has not yet, at least to my knowledge, discovered what it is that it wants out of the past. I would probably even argue that during the 20th century there occurred in nearly all Western and non-Western countries a definitive break with the evolution of the past and that therefore the return to an artificially created past is particularly destructive, because it is false both from the point of view of the past and the needs of today.

A second reason for my position that the historian has little to contribute to the contemporary effort to create a meaningful Muslim environment is that the historian, whether antiquarian, diachronist, or diatopist, is, at this time, for the most part not a Muslim. Even if he is technically one, his training and his values derive from a Western type of scientific inquiry, a type which is not wrong or immoral by itself, but which is not attuned to the needs and expectations of today's Muslim world. The historian will be able to help whenever questions will be asked of him, which he is competent to answer. He is competent in dealing with restorations, and he is competent in explaining the development of the dome; he is even competent in defining the nature of symbols or of piety or of behaviour in the 13th or the 17th centuries, but he cannot say what any of them should be today and what their architectural expression may be.

To sum up, I would like to argue:
1. that the historian can only react to questions given to him by the contemporary world; I have not seen or heard anything more profound than either "there was a glorious past, let us make a great future but not in the same way", or "drown us in forms, give us clues for significant signs"; I have not heard deeper queries about contemporary quests or contemporary techniques that would make me feel that my knowledge of the past can be anything but quaint and cute;
2. even if cultural values remain traditional (or Muslim lands wish to maintain them as such, with whatever variants are introduced from country to country), techniques and material aspirations have been revolutionised in the past 50 years to the point that the architectural past is no more relevant than the horse and buggy; knowledge of history can help in developing culture and pride or self-esteem, but not in creating architecture;
3. the historian will always remain the witness of what happened, even its interpreter, but not as an aide to creation;
4. the historian of anything has a role to play in generalising about the history he knows, but he is not equipped to deal with the needs of today.

* This is the text of a lecture delivered in 1995.

Oleg Grabar
Curriculum Vitae

Oleg Grabar was born on November 3, 1929, in Strasbourg, France. He received his secondary education at the Lycées Claude Bernard and Louis-le-Grand in Paris. He completed his undergraduate work both at the University of Paris and at Harvard University in 1950, where he studied ancient, medieval and modern history. He went on to Princeton University for his graduate work, where he received his PhD in Oriental Languages and Literatures and History of Art in 1955. While a graduate student, he spent the 1953–1954 academic year as a Fellow at the American School of Oriental Research in Jerusalem.

He started his teaching career at the University of Michigan, where he taught from 1954 to 1969, becoming a full professor in 1964. In 1969, he moved to Harvard University, where he was a Professor of Fine Arts until 1980, and then the first Aga Khan Professor of Islamic Art and Architecture. In 1990, he retired from Harvard University, where he continues to be an emeritus professor, to become a professor at the School of Historical Studies at the Institute for Advanced Study in Princeton. He retired from the Institute in 1998, where he is also an emeritus professor.

During his academic tenure at these three institutions, Oleg Grabar also took on other responsibilities. He served as the Director of the American School of Oriental Research in Jerusalem (1960–1961). He was the Near East editor for the journal *Ars Orientalis* (1957–1970) and an Honorary Curator of Near Eastern Art at the Smithsonian Institute's Freer Gallery of Art (1958–1969). In addition, he was the Secretary of the American Research Institute in Turkey (1964–1969), Vice President of the American School of Oriental Research (1967–1975), a member of the Executive Committees of the Max van Berchem Foundation in Geneva (1984–2000) and the American Academy of Arts and Sciences (1984–1988) and the founding editor of the journal *Muqarnas* (1979–1990). He was a Steering Committee member of the Aga Khan Award for Architecture from 1978 to 1988, and a member of the Master Jury for its 1989 cycle.

He has held lectureships at a number of universities and institutions including Columbia University, Oberlin College, New York University, the National Gallery in Washington, D.C., the Institut du Monde Arabe, the Ecole des Hautes Etudes en Sciences Sociales, the Collège de France, Florida State University, Indiana University and Bogazici Universitesi.

He is the recipient of numerous awards including the Charles L. Freer Medal for the Study of Asian Art in 2001, and the College Art Association's Annual Award for Excellence in 2004. In 2003, he was awarded an honorary Doctorate in Humane Letters from the University of Michigan.

He is the author of more than 30 books in English and French. These include *The Formation of Islamic Art* (New Haven: Yale University Press, 1973, 1987); *The Alhambra* (London: Penguin Books, 1978); *The Illustrations of the Maqamat* (Chicago: University of Chicago Press, 1984); *The Great Mosque of Isfahan* (New York: New York University Press, 1990); *The Mediation of Ornament* (Princeton: Princeton University Press, 1992); *The Shape of the Holy* (Princeton: Princeton University Press, 1996); *The Dome of the Rock* (with Saïd Nuseibeh) (Milan: Rizzoli, 1996); *Islamic Art and Architecture, 650–1250* (with M. Jenkins-Madina and the late R. Ettinghausen) (New Haven: Yale University Press, 2001); *The Dome of the Rock* (Cambridge: Harvard University Press, 2006); and *Masterpieces of Islamic Art: The Decorated Page from the 8th to the 17th Century* (New York and Munich: Prestel, 2009) Translations of his writings have appeared in Arabic, German, Turkish, Persian, Polish and Spanish. He is also the author of more than 100 articles. He has compiled over 80 of these in his four-volume work, *Constructing the Study of Islamic Art* (London: Ashgate, 2006).

Award Recipients
Project
Data

Wadi Hanifa Wetlands
Riyadh, Saudi Arabia

Project Data
Client **High Commission for the Development of Arriyadh Development Authority, Saudi Arabia:**
HRH Prince Salman bin Abdulaziz Al-Saud, Chairman of the High Commission for the Development of Arriyadh.
HRH Prince Sattam bin Abdulaziz Al-Saud, Deputy Chairman of the High Commission for the Development of Arriyadh.
Abdullatif bin Abdulmalik Al-Sheikh, Member of the High Commission for the Development of Arriyadhh and President of the Arriyadh Development Authority.

Landscape Architects **Moriyama & Teshima Planners Limited, Canada**
George Stockton, President
Consulting Engineers **Buro Happold, UK**
Roderick Macdonald, Chairman

Catchment Area **4,000 km² over a 120 km stretch**
Cost **US$ 160 million**
Design **2001 (and ongoing)**
Completed **2004–2007 (and ongoing)**

www.arriyadh.com

Bibliography
Arriyadh Development Authority/Moriyama & Teshima/Buro Happold, *Wadi Hanifa Comprehensive Development Plan* (October 2002)

Arriyadh Development Authority
The High Commission for the Development of Riyadh, chaired by HRH Prince Salman bin Abdulaziz Al-Saud, was established in 1974 (1394H). The High Commission oversees the economic, social, cultural, architectural, environmental and infrastructural development of the Saudi Arabian capital, and coordinates the activities of public and private organisations engaged in developments of the city.

The Arriyadh Development Authority (ADA) is the executive arm and implementing agency of the High Commission. It is responsible for instituting policies and procedures through comprehensive, strategic, long-term plans designed to raise the efficiency of the services and infrastructural facilities in the city and for the implementation of comprehensive development projects in Riyadh, with the ultimate goal of improving the living standards of its inhabitants.

The High Commission for the Development of Riyadh received the Aga Khan Award for Architecture in 1989 for the Al-Kindi Plaza and Hayy Assafarat Landscaping; in 1995 for the Great Mosque of Riyadh and Development of the Old City Centre; and in 1998 for the Tuwaiq Palace in Riyadh.

Moriyama & Teshima Planners Limited
Moriyama & Teshima is a Canadian architecture, planning and landscape architecture firm that has, over the past 30 years, built a body of landscapes and master plans for urban environments, ecological regions and entire watersheds. In 2001, the High Commission for the Development of Arriyadh commissioned the Joint Venture of Moriyama & Teshima Planners Limited and Buro Happold to develop a Comprehensive Development Plan for Wadi Hanifa.

Buro Happold
Buro Happold is an engineering, design, planning, project management and consulting services firm founded in 1976 in Bath, UK. The firm operates worldwide and in almost all areas of engineering for the built environment including buildings, infrastructure and environmental projects.

Revitalisation of the Hypercentre of Tunis
Tunis, Tunisia

Project Data
Client **Municipality of Tunis, Tunisia**
Architects **Association de Sauvegarde de la Médina de Tunis, Tunisia: Sémia Akrout-Yaïche, General Manager; Zoubeïr Mouhli, Deputy Director for Architecture and Urban Planning; Faïka Bejaoui, Deputy Director for Rehabilitation and Construction Permits; Abdelkerim Gazzah, Deputy Director of Restoration Works, Tunisia**
Mohsen Azaïez, Khaled Bouzid, Soulef Aouididi, Lassaâd Ben Slimene, Mourad Ghanoudi, Sadika Ghouma, Amel Meddeb-Ben Ghorbel, Khaled Ayed, Moez Jïed, Moez Tabib, Mehdi Ben Abdallah, project architects, Tunisia

Craftsmen **Safouane Ftouha, painter; Mongi Harbaoui, carpenter, Tunisia**

Site Area **Hypercentre: Around an axis 1,433 m long x 60 m wide (Avenue Habib Bourguiba and Avenue de France)**
Théâtre Municipal de Tunis **1,500 m²**
Marché Central **12,000 m²**
Ancien Tribunal administratif **2,530 m²**
Cinéma Palace **1,100 m²**

Cost **US$ 19.5 million**
Commission **1998**
Design **1994–2002**
Construction **1999–2007**
Occupancy **2007 (and ongoing)**

www.asmtunis.com

Bibliography
Zoubeïr Mouhli and Justin McGuinness, under the direction of Sémia Akrout-Yaïche and Viviane Bettaieb, *Médinances: Huit Visages de la Médina de Tunis* (Tunis, 1998).

Zoubeïr Mouhli and Justin McGuinness, under the direction of Sémia Akrout-Yaïche, *Tunis, 1800–1950. Portrait architectural et urbain* (Tunis, 2004).

Jean-Baptiste Minnaert, *Histoires d'architectures en Méditerranée XIXe-XXe siècles. Ecrire l'histoire d'un héritage bâti* (Paris, 2005).

Mohamed Awad, *Patrimoines partagés en Méditerranée. Eléments clés de la réhabilitation* (Programme Euromed Heritage II; Alexandria Preservation Trust, 2005).

Association de Sauvegarde de la Médina de Tunis
The Association de Sauvegarde de la Médina de Tunis (*Association for the Preservation of the Medina of Tunis*; ASM) was founded by the Tunis municipality in 1967. Its main purposes are to rehabilitate the image of the old city and to redefine the role of the old city within the urban agglomeration; to preserve the specificity and the unity of the historic city and to ensure its integration into the capital in order to prevent it from being marginalised. The ASM carries out its missions with the assistance of its architecture and planning unit and site team. In addition, the ASM serves as a meeting point and a research centre on urban, architectural and socioeconomic aspects of the old medina of Tunis. The ASM received an Aga Khan Award for Architecture in 1983 for the Hafsia Quarter; in 1989 for the Sidi el-Aloui Primary School; and in 1995 for the Reconstruction of the Hafsia Quarter II. Sémia Akrout-Yaïche, an architect and planner, has been Director General of the ASM since 1993.

Madinat al-Zahra Museum
Cordoba, Spain

Project Data
Client **Junta de Andalucía, Consejería de Cultura, Spain**

Architect **Nieto Sobejano Arquitectos, Spain:**
Fuensanta Nieto, Enrique Sobejano, partners in charge of design; Miguel Ubarrechena, project architect; Carlos Ballesteros, Pedro Quero, Juan Carlos Redondo, project team

Museological Concept and Programming **Antonio Vallejo Triano, Director of Madinat al-Zahra Archaeological Site, Spain**
Content Programming **Manuel Acién Almansa, Spain**

Site Supervisor **Miguel Mesas Izquierdo, Spain**
Structural Engineers **N.B.35. S.L., Spain**
Mechanical Engineers **Geasyt S.A., Spain**
Exhibition Design **Nieto Sobejano Arquitectos; Frade Arquitectos, Spain**
Museographic Production **Empty, S.L., Spain**
General Contractors **Ecasur 10, S.A., Ejuca, S.A., Spain**

Built Area **9,125 m²**
Site Area **53,897 m²**
Cost **US$ 20.7 million**
Commission **2001**
Design **2001–2003**
Construction **2005–2008**
Occupancy **2008**

www.juntadeandalucia.es/cultura/museos/CAMA
www.nietosobejano.com

Bibliography
Philip Jodidio, *Architecture Now! Museums* (Taschen, 2010).

Nieto Sobejano Arquitectos
Fuensanta Nieto and Enrique Sobejano trained as architects at the Escuela Técnica Superior de Arquitectura de Madrid (ETSAM) in Spain and the Graduate School of Architecture, Planning and Preservation at Columbia University in New York. They are founding partners of Nieto Sobejano Arquitectos, with offices in Madrid and Berlin. Fuensanta Nieto is professor at the School of Architecture of Universidad Europea de Madrid, and Enrique Sobejano is professor of architecture at the Universität der Künste Berlin. Both have been visiting critics and lecturers at several international universities and institutions. From 1986 to 1991 they were directors of the architectural journal *Arquitectura*, edited by Colegio Oficial de Arquitectos de Madrid. Their work has been published in many international magazines and books and has been exhibited at the Biennale di Venezia (2000, 2002 and 2006) and at the Museum of Modern Art in New York (2006). They have been awarded the Spanish National Prize for Restoration (2008). Nieto Sobejano Arquitectos recently completed the Moritzburg Museum in Halle (Germany); their projects under construction include the Contemporary Arts Center in Córdoba, Spain, and the Joanneum Museum in Graz, Austria.

Ipekyol Textile Factory
Edirne, Turkey

Project Data
Client **Ipekyol Giyim Sanayi; Yalçın Ayaydın, Chairman, Turkey**

Architect **EAA – Emre Arolat Architects, Emre Arolat, Turkey**
Gonca Paşolar, Eda Yazkurt, Ertuğrul Morçöl, Meltem Emden, Ekin Erik, Gulseren Gerede Tecim, project team, Turkey

Contractor and Structural Engineer **Turin Turizm İnşaat ve Ticaret A.Ş., Turkey**
Mechanical Engineer **Toptas Mekanik Tesisat Sanayi, Turkey**
Electrical Engineer **Truva Elektrik Makine Ltd.Şti., Turkey**

Built area **20,000 m²**
Cost **US$ 16.5 million**
Commission **2004**
Design **2004–2005**
Construction **2005–2006**
Occupancy **2006**

www.emrearolat.com

EAA – Emre Arolat Architects
EAA – Emre Arolat Architects was founded in May 2004 by Emre Arolat and Gonca Paşolar in Istanbul—a continuation of Emre Arolat's architectural practices that started when he joined Arolat Architects as an Associate Designer in 1987. EAA – Emre Arolat Architects has a wide range of projects and a professional architectural staff in two different offices in Istanbul. The other partners in the practice are Neşet Arolat, Şaziment Arolat, Kerem Piker and Sezer Bahtiyar.
Emre Arolat was born in Ankara in 1963 and received his bachelor's and master's degrees in Architecture at Mimar Sinan University (1986 and 1992). He worked as an Assistant Architect at Metcalf and Associates Architectural Office in Washington, D.C., between 1986 and 1987, and as an Associate Designer and Senior Partner at Arolat Architects (1987 to 2004). In addition to his architectural practice, he has taught architectural design studios and served on project juries at several universities in Turkey.

Bridge School
Xiashi, Fujian Province, China

Project Data
Client **Xiashi Village; Shi Xiu Qing, village head, China**
Local government of Pinghe County, Fujian; Hong Lizhuan, County Leader; Zhang Guoyang, Party Secretary; Zeng QingFeng, County Official, China

Architect **Li Xiaodong Atelier: Li Xiaodong, principal architect; Li Ye, Chuan Wang, Qiong Liang, Mengjia Liu and Junqi Nie, project team, China**

Collaborator **Hedao Architecture Design, Xiamen, Fujian, China**
Project Manager **Chen Jiansheng, China**
Structural Engineer **Li Xiaodong (concept); Hedao Architecture Design (construction drawing), China**

Contractor **Zhangzhou Steel; Minqbiao Ma, manager, China**

Built Area **240 m²**
Site Area **1,550 m²**
Building height **6.5 m**
Cost **US$ 100,000**
Commission **2007**
Design **2008**
Construction **2008**
Occupancy **2008**

www.lixiaodong.net

Li Xiaodong Atelier
Li Xiaodong is a practicing architect, educator and researcher on architecture. He graduated from the School of Architecture at Tsinghua University (1984) and received his PhD from the School of Architecture, Delft/Eindhoven University of Technology (1993). He established Li Xiaodong Atelier in 1997. His design work ranges from interiors and architecture to urban spaces. His work has won national and international design awards in China, Germany, the United States and the Netherlands.
Li Xiaodong has received international recognition for his teaching, including an RIBA tutor's prize (2000) and SARA tutor's prize (2001) from the Department of Architecture at the National University of Singapore. He is currently chair of the architecture programme at the School of Architecture at Tsinghua University, in Beijing. His research and publications, including articles and books in both Chinese and English, cover a wide range of subjects: cultural studies, history and theory of architecture and urban studies.

Shortlisted Projects

AUB Campus Master Plan
Beirut, Lebanon
Architect **Sasaki Associates, Machado & Silvetti Associates**
Client **American University of Beirut**
Design **2001–2002**
Completed **2007–ongoing**
Site Area **240,000 m²**
Charles Holster Centre **20,400 m²**
Olayan School of Business **12,542 m²**

Women's Health Centre
Ouagadougou, Burkina Faso
Architect **FARE Studio, Riccardo Vanucci; ANSWER Architectes, Dieudonné Wango**
Client **AIDOS (Associazione Italiana Donne per lo Sviluppo), Daniel Colomba; Voix de Femmes, Mariam Laminzana Traoré**
Design **2005**
Completed **2007**
Built Area **500 m²**
Site Area **1,600 m²**

Green School
Badung, Bali, Indonesia
Architect **PT Bambu, Aldo Landwehr, John Hardy**
Client **PT Bambu**
Design **2006**
Completed **2007**
Site Area **103,143 m²**
Built Area **7,542 m²**

Chandgaon Mosque
Chittagong, Bangladesh
Architect **Urbana, Kashef Mahboob Chowdhury**
Client **Faisal M. Khan**
Design **2006**
Completed **2007**
Built Area **1,048 m²**
Site Area **5,200 m²**

Nishorgo Oirabot Nature Interpretation Centre
Teknaf, Bangladesh
Architect **Vitti Sthapati Brindo Ltd., Ehsan Khan**
Client **Ministry of Environment & Forest Bon Bhaban, Md. Ishtiaque Ahmed**
Design **2006**
Completed **2008**
Built Area **288 m²**

Restoration of Rubber Smokehouse
Kedah, Malaysia
Architect **Arkitek LLA, Laurence Loh**
Client **Loh Hock Joo**
Sponsor **DiGi Communications**
Design **2006–2007**
Completed **2007**
Site Area **1,803 m²**
Built Area **438 m²**

Tulou Collective Housing
Guangzhou, China
Architect **URBANUS Architecture & Design, Liu Xiaodu, Meng Yan**
Client **Shenhzen Vanke Real Estate Co. Ltd.**
Design **2006**
Completed **2008**
Site Area **9,141 m²**
Built Area **13,711 m²**

Palmyra House
Alibagh, India
Architect **Studio Mumbai Architects, Bijoy Jain**
Client **Jamshyd Sethna**
Design **2005–2006**
Completed **2007**
Built Area **277 m²**

Dowlat II Residential Building
Tehran, Iran
Architect **Arsh Design Studio,**
Ali Reza Sherafati, Rambid Eilkhani,
Panta Eslami, Nashid Nabian
Client **Ali Nazemian**
Design **2005–2006**
Completed **2007**
Built Area **535 m²**

Yodakandyia Community Centre
Hambantota District, Sri Lanka
Architect **Architecture for Humanity,**
Susi Jane Platt
Sponsor **UN Habitat, I.A. Hameed**
Client **Pinsara Federation of Community**
Development Councils
Design **2006**
Completed **2007**
Site Area **15,165 m²**
Built Area **894 m²**

Reconstruction of
Ngibikan Village
Yogyakarta, Indonesia
Architect **Eko Prawoto; Maryono,**
Community Leader
Client **Ngibikan Village Community**
Design **2006**
Completed **2006**
Site Area **43,255 m²**
Built Area **2,808 m²**

Souk Waqif
Doha, Qatar
Architect **Private Engineering Office,**
Mohamed Ali Abdullah
Client **Amiri Diwan**
Design **2004–2007**
Completed **2008**
Site Area **164,000 m²**

Conservation of Gjirokastra
Gjirokastra, Albania
Architect **Technical Team of**
Gjirokastra Conservation &
Development Organisation
Client **Gjirokastra Conservation &**
Development Organisation
Design **2001–ongoing**
Completed **2002–ongoing**
Site Area **785,000 m²**
Zekate House **484 m²**
Seven Fountains Hammam and Square
230 m²
Bazaar **4140 m²**
Castle of Gjirokastra **24,000 m²**
Omarate House **180 m²**

Rehabilitation of
Al-Karaouine Mosque
Fez, Morocco
Architect **Mohammed Fikri Ben Abdallah,**
Alae Bouayad
Client **Ministère des Habous et des**
Affaires Islamiques, Abdelaziz Derouiche
Design **2004–2005**
Completed **2007**
Site Area **7,200 m²**

Steering Committee

His Highness the Aga Khan
Chairman

Mohammad al-Asad
Architect and architectural historian; Chairman, Center for the Study of the Built Environment, Amman, Jordan

Homi K. Bhabha
Cultural theoretician; Anne F. Rothenberg Professor of the Humanities, Department of English, and Director of the Humanities Center, Harvard University, USA

Norman Foster
Architect; Chairman, Foster + Partners, UK

Glenn Lowry
Art historian; Director, Museum of Modern Art, New York, USA

Rahul Mehrotra
Architect; Principal, RMA Architects, Mumbai, India, and Professor and Chair, Department of Urban Planning and Design, Harvard University, USA

Mohsen Mostafavi
Architect; Dean, Graduate School of Design, Harvard University, USA

Farshid Moussavi
Architect; Partner, Foreign Office Architects, London, and Professor in Practice of Architecture, Harvard University, USA

Han Tümertekin
Architect; Principal, Mimarlar Tasarim Danismanlik Ltd., Istanbul, Turkey

Master Jury

Souleymane Bachir Diagne
Philosopher; Professor, Department of Philosophy, Columbia University, USA

Omar Abdulaziz Hallaj
Architect; Chief Executive Officer, Syria Trust for Development

Salah M. Hassan
Art historian and curator; Director of Africana Studies and Research Center, Cornell University, USA

Faryar Javaherian
Architect and curator; Co-founder of Gamma Consultants, Iran

Anish Kapoor
Artist, UK

Yu Kongjian
Landscape architect and urbanist; Founder and dean of Graduate School of Landscape Architecture, Peking University, China

Jean Nouvel
Architect; Founding Partner, Ateliers Jean Nouvel, France

Alice Rawsthorn
Design Critic, *International Herald Tribune*, UK

Basem Shihabi
Architect; Managing Partner, Omrania & Associates, Saudi Arabia

On-Site Project Reviewers

Sultan Barakat
Architect and academic; Professor in Politics at the University of York, UK

Hanif Kara
Structural engineer; Co-founder of Adams Kara Taylor (AKT), UK

Gökhan Karakuş
Designer, architectural critic and theorist; Founder of elmedya design studio, Istanbul, Turkey

Michele Lamprakos
Architect; Founder of PALIMPSEST design and consulting, USA

Kevin Mark Low
Architect; Founder of smallprojects, Kuala Lumpur, Malaysia

Yasser Mahgoub
Architect; Assistant Professor of Architecture, Kuwait University, Kuwait

Fuad H. Mallick
Architect; Chair of Department of Architecture at BRAC University, Dhaka, Bangladesh

Hassan Radoine
Architect; Chair of Architectural Engineering department, University of Sharjah, UAE

Wael Samhouri
Architect and urban designer; Architect in private practice and Chair of Architecture department, International University for Science and Technology, Damascus, Syria

May Shaer
Conservation architect working with the UNESCO-Iraq Office in Amman, Jordan

Brigitte Shim
Architect; Partner, Shim-Sutcliffe Architects, and Professor of Architecture, Landscape, and Design, University of Toronto, Canada

Amine Turki
Architect; Founder and chairman of the ITQAN Consortium and Secretary General of the Board of Architects, Tunisia

2010 Award Steering Committee and Master Jury
Seated, left to right: Faryar Javaherian, Norman Foster, Farshid Moussavi, Prince Hussain Aga Khan,
His Highness the Aga Khan, Princess Khaliya Aga Khan, Omar Abdulaziz Hallaj, Alice Rawsthorn, Homi K. Bhabha
Standing left to right: Han Tümertekin, Mohammad al-Asad, Souleymane Bachir Diagne, Yu Kongjian, Glenn Lowry,
Basem Shihabi, Salah M. Hassan, Rahul Mehrotra, Farrokh Derakhshani

Recipients of the Aga Khan Award for Architecture 1980–2010
Asia
Landscaping Integration of the Soekarno-Hatta Airport, Cengkareng, Indonesia, 1992
Kampung Kali Cho-de, Yogyakarta, Indonesia, 1992
Citra Niaga Urban Development, Samarinda, Indonesia, 1989
Kampung Kebalen Improvement, Surabaya, Indonesia, 1986
Saïd Naum Mosque, Jakarta, Indonesia, 1986
Pondok Pesantren Pabelan, Central Java, Indonesia, 1980
Kampung Improvement Programme, Jakarta, Indonesia, 1980
Moulmein Rise Residential Tower, Singapore, Singapore, 2007
University of Technology Petronas, Bandar Seri Iskandar, Malaysia, 2007
Petronas Towers, Kuala Lumpur, Malaysia, 2004
Datai Hotel, Pulau Langkawi, Malaysia, 2001
Salinger Residence, Selangor, Malaysia, 1998
Menara Mesiniaga, Kuala Lumpur, Malaysia, 1992
Tanjong Jara Beach Hotel, Kuala Terranganu, Malaysia, 1983
Bridge School, Xiashi, Fujian Province, China, 2010
School in Rudrapur, Rudrapur, Bangladesh, 2007
Grameen Bank Housing Programme, various locations, Bangladesh, 1989
National Assembly Building, Sher-e-Bangla Nagar, Dhaka, Bangladesh, 1989
Vidhan Bhavan, Bhopal, India, 1998
Slum Networking of Indore, Indore, India, 1998
Lepers Hospital, Chopda Taluka, India, 1998
Aranya Community Housing, Indore, India, 1992
Entrepreneurship Development Institute of India, Ahmedabad, India, 1992
Mughal Sheraton Hotel, Agra, India, 1980
Alhamra Arts Council, Lahore, Pakistan, 1998
Khuda-ki-Basti Incremental Development Scheme, Hyderabad, Pakistan, 1992
Bhong Mosque, Rahim-Yar Khan, Pakistan, 1986
Tomb of Shah Rukn-i-'Alam, Multan, Pakistan, 1983
Restoration of Bukhara Old City, Bukhara, Uzbekistan, 1992
Bagh-e-Ferdowsi, Tehran, Iran, 2001
New Life for Old Structures, various locations, Iran, 2001
Shushtar New Town, Shushtar, Iran, 1986
Ali Qapu, Chehel Sutun and Hasht Behesht, Isfahan, Iran, 1980
Stone Building System, Dar'a Province, Syria, 1992
Azem Palace, Damascus, Syria, 1983
Samir Kassir Square, Beirut, Lebanon, 2007
Great Omari Mosque, Sidon, Lebanon, 1989
Old City of Jerusalem Revitalisation Programme, Jerusalem, 2004
Al-Aqsa Mosque, al-Haram al-Sharif, Jerusalem, 1986
Rehabilitation of Hebron Old Town, Hebron, Palestine, 1998
SOS Children's Village, Aqaba, Jordan, 2001
East Wahdat Upgrading Programme, Amman, Jordan, 1992
National Museum, Doha, Qatar, 1980
Water Towers, Kuwait City, Kuwait, 1980
Wadi Hanifa Wetlands, Riyadh, Saudi Arabia, 2010
Tuwaiq Palace, Riyadh, Saudi Arabia, 1998
Great Mosque and Redevelopment of the Old City Centre, Riyadh, Saudi Arabia, 1992
Al-Kindi Plaza, Riyadh, Saudi Arabia, 1989
Hayy Assafarat Landscaping, Riyadh, Saudi Arabia, 1989
Ministry of Foreign Affairs, Riyadh, Saudi Arabia, 1989
Corniche Mosque, Jeddah, Saudi Arabia, 1989
Hajj Terminal, King Abdul Aziz International Airport, Jeddah, Saudi Arabia, 1983
Inter-Continental Hotel and Conference Centre, Mecca, Saudi Arabia, 1980
Rehabilitation of the City of Shibam, Shibam, Yemen, 2007
Restoration of the Amiriya Complex, Rada, Yemen, 2007
Restoration of Al-Abbas Mosque, Asnaf, Yemen, 2004
Conservation of Old Sana'a, Sana'a, Yemen, 1992

Africa
Bibliotheca Alexandrina, Alexandria, Egypt, 2004
Nubian Museum, Aswan, Egypt, 2001
Cultural Park for Children, Cairo, Egypt, 1992
Ismaïlliya Development Projects, Ismaïliyya, Egypt, 1986
Ramses Wissa Wassef Arts Centre, Giza, Egypt, 1983
Darb Qirmiz Quarter, Cairo, Egypt, 1983
Halawa House, Agamy, Egypt, 1980
Royal Netherlands Embassy, Addis Ababa, Ethiopia, 2007
Central Market, Koudougou, Burkina Faso, 2007
Primary School, Gando, Burkina Faso, 2004
Panafrican Institute of Development, Ouagadougou, Burkina Faso, 1992
Kahere Eila Poultry Farming School, Koliagbe, Guinea, 2001
Great Mosque of Niono, Niono, Mali, 1983
Medical Centre, Mopti, Mali, 1980
Yaama Mosque, Tahoua, Niger, 1986
Alliance Franco-Sénégalaise, Kaolack, Senegal, 1992
Agricultural Training Centre, Nianing, Senegal, 1980
Kaedi Regional Hospital, Kaedi, Mauritania, 1992
Aït Iktel, Abadou, Morocco, 2001
Rehabilitation of Asilah, Asilah, Morocco, 1989
Dar Lamane Housing, Casablanca, Morocco, 1986
Courtyard Houses, Agadir, Morocco, 1980
Revitalisation of the Hypercentre of Tunis, Tunisia, 2010
Kairouan Conservation Programme, Kairouan, Tunisia, 1992
Hafsia Quarter II, Tunis, Tunisia, 1992
Sidi el-Aloui Primary School, Tunis, Tunisia, 1989
Hafsia Quarter I, Tunis, Tunisia, 1983
Résidence Andalous, Sousse, Tunisia, 1983
Sidi Bou Saïd, Tunis, Tunisia, 1980

Europe
Institut du Monde Arabe, Paris, France, 1989
Madinat al-Zahra Museum, Cordoba, Spain, 2010
Rehabilitation of the Walled City, Nicosia, Cyprus, 2007
Mostar Old Town, Mostar, Bosnia-Herzegovina, 1986
Sherefudin's White Mosque, Visoko, Bosnia-Herzegovina, 1983
Ipekyol Textile Factory, Edirne, Turkey, 2010
B2 House, Ayvacik, Turkey, 2004
Olbia Social Centre, Antalya, Turkey, 2001
Palace Parks Programme, Istanbul, Turkey, 1992
Demir Holiday Village, Bodrum, Turkey, 1992
Mosque of the Grand National Assembly, Ankara, Turkey, 1992
Re-Forestation Programme of the Middle East Technical University, Ankara, Turkey, 1992
Gürel Family Summer Residence, Çanakkale, Turkey, 1989
Social Security Complex, Istanbul, Turkey, 1986
Historic Sites Development, Istanbul, Turkey, 1986
Nail Çakirhan House, Akyaka Village, Turkey, 1983
Turkish Historical Society, Ankara, Turkey, 1980
Rüstem Pasha Caravenserai, Edirne, Turkey, 1980
Ertegün House, Bodrum, Turkey, 1980

Worldwide
Sandbag Shelter Prototypes, various locations worldwide, 2004

Acknowledgements
This monograph has been conceived by Mohammad Al-Asad, Mohsen Mostafavi and Farrokh Derakhshani on behalf of the Steering Committee of the 2010 Aga Khan Award for Architecture, in collaboration with Prince Hussain Aga Khan.

Texts were edited by Melissa Vaughn; Stephen Ramos compiled materials for the project descriptions from reports prepared by the 2010 on-site project reviewers.

The visual materials of this volume have been compiled by Nadia Siméon.

Graphic Design
Irma Boom

Printing and Binding
Kösel, Altusried-Krugzell, Germany

Published by
Lars Müller Publishers
Baden, Switzerland
www.lars-muller-publishers.com

© 2011 The Aga Khan Award for Architecture and Lars Müller Publishers

All rights reserved. Except for brief quotations in a review, this book, or any part thereof, may not be reproduced, stored in or introduced into a retrieval system, or transmitted, in any form or by any means, electronic, mechanical, photocopying, recording or otherwise, without the prior written permission of the publisher.

ISBN 978-3-03778-242-2

A full CIP record for this book is available from the British Library
A full CIP record is available from the Library of Congress
Library of Congress Catalog Card Number: available

Aga Khan Award for Architecture
P.O. Box 2049
1211 Geneva 2
Switzerland

www.akaa.org

Photo Credits
Fernando Alda: 66–67; Amir Anoushfar: 254–261; Arriyadh Development Authority: 26–27, 34–43, 284–285; Arsh Design Studio: 190–193; Association de Sauvegarde de la Médina de Tunis: 222; Jacques Bétant: 314–315; Chen Jiansheng: 88–89; Anne de Henning: 236–237; Cemal Emden: 2–3, 20–21, 60–65, 68–71, 144–145, 148–149, 280–281, 290–291; Gjirokastra Conservation and Development Organisation: 244–247; Courtesy of Oleg Grabar: 304, 308–311, 316–321, 329, 335; Rayya Haddad: 48–53; Ahkamul Hakim: 99, 106, 107, 206–209; BKS Inan: 110–119, 124–131; Alket Islami: 242–243; Baan Iwan: 169; Salah Jabeur: 8–9, 216–221, 224–227, 272–273; Li Xiaodong: 16–17, 76–87, 266–267; Christopher Little: 312–313; Thomas Mayer: 138–143, 146–147; Cariddi Nardulli: 92–93; Eko Prawoto: 205; Bas Princen: 94–97; PT Bambu: 104–105; Hassan Radoine: 223; Wael Samhouri: 188–189; Sasaki Associates: 45–47; Ziyad Shawkat: 232–237; Kristian Skeie: 346–347; Rajesh Vora: 174–183; Melissa Walsh: 152–157; Eresh Weerasuriya: 196–201; Yang Chaoying: 164–168, 170–171.

Drawings
All drawings are supplied by the architects except the one on page 239, which is from Richard Andrew, Carden & Godfrey Architects.

Additional illustrations, videos and information about the 2010 projects and other background materials is available at www.akdn.org/architecture

Aga Khan Trust for Culture
Sirwan Abdulaziz
Shiraz Allibhai
Aurélie Charlet
Luis Monreal
Van Nguyen
William O'Reilly
Sam Pickens
Ibai Rigby
Thê-Hông Tang-Lâm
Cécile Thiery

Award Secretariat
Nuha Ansari
Francesca Cantien
Farrokh Derakhshani
Anna Grichting
Nadia Siméon
Marie-Martine de Techtermann

Documentation Assistance
Saman Abdulaziz
Jeffrey Allen
Philippa Baker
Khadija Buhadi
Donnathea Campbell
Katie Inglis
El Hadi Jazairy
Gulguna Mukairshoeva
Mina Safai
Cyrus Samii
Deen Sharp
Christine Thiên Kim Tang
Cong-Thien Tang

2010 Award Regional Coordinators
Fay Cheah
Francis Diebedo Kéré
Samia Rab
Budi Sukada
Bahrom Yusupov

2010 Award Cycle Contributors
Kamran Adle
Zainab Faruqui Ali
Richard Bödeker
Joan Busquets
Selin Cinar
Darab Diba
Banu Durmuşoğlu
Antoni Folkers
Maximillian Jacobson-Gonzales
Khadija Jamal-Shaban
Renata Holod
Romi Khosla
Laurence Liauw
David Nelson
Setareh Ordoobadi
Suha Özkan
Nasser O. Rabbat
Hashim Sarkis
Yildirim Yavuz
and
823 nominators
472 project architects

Implicate & Explicate